ALLEN FISHER was born i[...] poetry since 1962. A printer, [...] he has produced over eighty ch[...] graphics and art documentation[...] and lives and lectures in Hereford. He has exhibited paintings in many shows and examples of his work are in the Tate Gallery collection. Amongst his books are: *Bavuska* (1969), *Before Ideas, Ideas* (1971), *Place* (various books 1974–81), *The Apocalyptic Sonnets* (1978), *Poetry for Schools* (1980), *Blood Bone Brain* (1982), *Unpolished Mirrors* (1985), *Brixton Fractals* (1985), and *Buzzards and Bees* (1987).

BILL GRIFFITHS was born in London, north of the river, in 1948. He sees himself as a quiet and unassuming guy, and is at a loss to explain why he finds himself continually surrounded by unexpected dangers and adventures. The poems may hold a clue, exhibiting a euphoric indulgence in group identity and a tribal affinity with clearly inanimate objects. In the early 1970s he started up a little press, Pirate Press, publishing mostly his own work, sometimes the work of other young poets, and sometimes translations of pre-modern poetry. The selection of work presented here covers booklets from the 1970s and 80s; most were published originally by Pirate Press in conjunction with Writers Forum, some by other little presses like Galloping Dog, New London Pride, and Spectacular Diseases; other poems appeared first in little magazines like *Poetry Review* (under the editorship of Eric Mottram), *Second Æon* and *Figs*.

BRIAN CATLING was born in 1948 in London, where he still lives. His publications include *The First Electron Heresy*, *Vorticegarden*, *Pleiades in Nine* (Albion Village Press); *Tulpa Index* (St George Press, Norwich School of Art); *Boschlog* (A Few Goats Press, New York). He is a sculptor and performance artist whose most recent solo shows have been at the Neuw Gallerie, Aachen; Matts Gallery, London; and the Museum of Modern Art, Oxford.

He is principal lecturer in the sculpture department at Brighton Polytechnic, tutor in sculpture at the Royal College of Art, and guest professor to the Vestlandets Kunstakademi, Bergen.

Allen Fisher, Bill Griffiths
& Brian Catling

FUTURE
EXILES

3 LONDON POETS

Paladin Re/Active Anthology No. 1

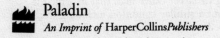

Paladin
An Imprint of HarperCollinsPublishers

Paladin
An Imprint of HarperCollins*Publishers*
77–85 Fulham Palace Road,
Hammersmith, London W6 8JB

A Paladin Paperback Original 1992
9 8 7 6 5 4 3 2 1

ISBN 0 586 09078 9

Set in Bembo

Printed in Great Britain by
HarperCollinsManufacturing Glasgow

Acknowledgements

Allen Fisher

Played Against Drum-Beats (first published in *Perfect Bound*, Cambridge, 1976)

Enclosed Delight (first published in *Curtains*, Hebden Bridge, 1976)

Cleopatra's Sonority (first published in *Poetry for Schools*, Aloes Books, London, 1980)

Gripping the Rail (first published as a chapbook with *Clasp Flow Other*, Pig Press, Durham, 1977)

All of *Shorting-Out* (first published in book form as *Poetry for Schools*, Aloes Books, London, 1980)

The Mathematics of Rimbaud (first published in *Reality Studios*, Vol. 2 No. 3, London, 1980)

Ideas on the Culture Dreamed Of (Spanner, London, 1982)

Brixton Fractals (Aloes Books, London, 1985)

Banda (first published in *The Beau*, Dublin, 1985)

African Boog (first published with other poems in the chapbook *African Boog*, Ta'wil Books, London, 1983)

Bel Air (first published in *Sulfur 12*, California, 1985)

Birdland (first published in *Sow's Ear*, Stafford, 1985)

Buzzards and Bees (Microbrigade, London, 1986)

Break-a-Leg (first published in *Angel Exhaust*, London 1987)

Breaks (first published in *Talus*, London, 1987)

Boogie Woogie (first published in *Sink*, California, 1986)

Bop (first published in *Paris Exiles*, Paris, 1986)

Cakewalk (first published in *Reality Studios*, London, 1988)

Camel Walk (first published as a broadsheet, Spanner, London, 1988)

Bill Griffiths

Some of the poems printed here have previously appeared in little
press publications from: Anarcho Press (London), Arc Publications
(Todmorden), Coach House Press (Toronto), Galloping Dog
Press (Newcastle), New London Pride, Spectacular Diseases
(Peterborough), and Writers Forum (London); and in magazines
including *Poetry Review* (under the editorship of Eric Mottram) and
Figs (edited by Tony Baker).

Brian Catling

Vorticegarden (1974) and *Pleiades In Nine* (1976) were first published by the Albion Village Press
Das Kranke Tier (1976) and *Vox Humana* (1977) were first published by Otto Stanton
Tulpa Index (1983) was first published by St George Press, Norwich School of Art

Allen Fisher

GRAVITY AS A CONSEQUENCE OF SHAPE

Contents

The Necessary Business of Allen Fisher

I must create a system, or be enslaved by another man's;
I will not reason or compare; my business is to create.

WILLIAM BLAKE

'Perfection. Constancy. Consistency.' For many contemporary poets, these three words might constitute a thumbnail manifesto for the creation of complete verbal icons. For a poet like Allen Fisher they are 'terms applicable to a static state of affairs' which he must reject and, what is more, he often explicitly embraces their opposites.

His first published work, *Thomas Net's Tree-Birst* (1966–70) is a useful signpost to Fisher's mature work: it consists entirely of a text made by the deletion of letters and phrases from Wordsworth's *The Prelude*. As such it declares his distance from mainstream literary culture and asserts a streak of vital irreverence. More importantly, it was not a work of self-expression but a set project with a certain procedure. Fisher does characteristically work at the level of projects, by setting himself large objectives and limits with a particular method. Partly as a result of this, and partly because of his extraordinary energy, Fisher's output in the 1970s and 1980s has been furious, no less as a painter, performance artist, theorist and little press publisher than as a poet. The result is a series of heterogeneous, overlapping works, initially overwhelming in their bulk and baffling in their complexity, but eventually surprising in their methodologies and sweeping in their scope. They represent the most serious and extensive attempt to register late-twentieth-century realities at the level of both form and content in British poetry today.

It is good that this work is being published outside of the little presses at last, though it is not surprising that Fisher has been largely ignored by the literary establishment. When its own poetry is limited to bland narratives or metaphorical excess, tailored to the creative writing class or to poetry competitions, how could it begin to accept what he does *as* poetry? For Fisher, poetry is repeatedly defined by a set of paradigms that must continuously be broken in an endless but unpredictable setting up and breaking of rules.

In 1975, when Fisher was still only thirty-one, he stopped to take stock of his work to date in *Prosyncel* which, with characteristic humour, he described as a 'blueprint for a retrospective catalogue'. It listed thirty-four projects in progress, varying in originality and profundity as well as in style. Unfortunately none of this work is in the present collection. On the one hand Fisher attempted to explore all kinds of information, scientific and mathematical as well as cultural. (He began a degree in mathematics about this time, later abandoned. In the 1980s he studied art history, a subject he now teaches.) On the other hand he was assimilating every avant-garde technique. *Prosyncel* itemises collages, found texts, mail art, dream poems; there were experiments in process music and conceptual art; there were performances which were part of the collective *Fluxus England West*; there were graphic works and photographic works, and collaborative writings. Some of the works favoured strict procedures, others a radical discontinuity. What was coming to the fore during this period of experiment was Fisher's desire to show his working processes in the work itself and to subvert them and undermine the authoritarian nature of systems by his interventions. (What else could a radical poet do but intervene if a randomly selected list of words suddenly spelt out a racist slogan?) Simultaneously the role of the ego of the author – still the validating centre of most contemporary verse – is undermined by the use of such systems.

Also in 1975, Allen Fisher received the Alice Hunt Bartlett
Award from the Poetry Society for the first volume of one of
the thirty-four projects, *Place*, a poetic achievement of some
magnitude which was to occupy him during the rest of the
decade. Since the present selection dates mainly from the 1980s,
it might be useful to describe this project. Its central concern
is with the poet's own reading on locality and history and
the transformation of this. This material provides information,
'resources' and quotations that are offered not as evidence
of a case, as quotations are in essays, but are part of the
work's 'shading', the co-existence of often mutually cancelling
cross-references between its five parts. They contribute not to a
unity of meaning (*a* meaning for the work) but to an expansive
presentation of various meanings. However, at a local level the
text can simply trace London historically as a record of its own
research:

1583	When we went our perambulation at Vicar's Oke in Rogation week	£0.2s.6d
1704	Paid for 100lbs cheese, spent at Vicar's Oke	£0.8s.0d
1973	Bus fare back from search for Vicar's Oak	£0.60p

The work is therefore learned in a curiously offhand way,
and as knowingly self-contradictory as Whitman's, though the
figures of Blake, Ezra Pound and Charles Olson also stand
behind it. *Place* has less a fixed procedure, the working through
of a system, than an ongoing process (Fisher uses the term
'processual'), one in which Fisher deliberately intervenes, adding
extra sections as he desires. The results of the project were
published in four large volumes, with a number of subsidiary
pamphlets. Fisher hoped that readers could join it at any point
equally validly, like joining the surface of a moving sphere.

> the centre moves   continues to
> move
> us   many centres
> ecumenopolis
> and
> or the loci of a point on a moving sphere
>
>   I who am where I am
>   feel the surges of
>   of the pulses that are
>   not my heart's

As can be seen, the thematic concerns with place are both environmental and psychosomatic, with the interrelation of individual organism, mind, place and community mainly focused upon London, where Fisher has lived most of his life.

The final part of *Place*, 'Unpolished Mirrors', surprisingly adopts the oracular style of Blakean monologue, with narrators ranging from the Gardener, who is responsible for the 'garden of a coming English Revolution', to the repressive tyrant, Watling. London becomes similarly mythical, although there is a continued concern for both environmental and cultural 'memory', and for the dream of that English Revolution: 'an unhinged garden door/the dreamscape remaining beyond'.

Place is one of the few works to attempt to map what London might mean, and to use a method adequate to that complexity. As with the city itself, you find your way around the work.

In the 1980s Fisher kept a number of projects going simultaneously (with his painting increasingly preoccupying him) but one still progressing project, *Gravity as a consequence of shape*, has produced his finest work, and it is this work that fills sections 5–8 of this selection. The writing is denser and more demanding than *Place* and the condensed reference and poetic use of specialist languages found in the poetry of J.H. Prynne combines with the juxtapositions and leaps favoured by a writer like Tom Raworth. The excitement of these texts lies in the tension between the forward thrust and the lateral shifts, which creates a jagged polyphony:

> The quantum leap
> between some lines
> so wide
> it hurts.

Fisher's own introduction to his thinking just prior to beginning the project, 'The Mathematics of Rimbaud' is published here. Like other serious twentieth-century writers he has sought structural homologies in the sciences. *Gravity as a consequence of shape* began as an investigation of perception and consciousness, and its title reveals Fisher's interest in the mapping of contours. 'The simply beautiful morning conceals the complexity of perception,' Fisher notes, and in *Gravity* nothing is taken for granted. By fracturing different kinds of systematised knowledge and then rearranging them, he is miming the processes of the interaction of consistent memory and inventive memory (terms explained in 'The Mathematics of Rimbaud' and used in 'Around the World'). He is also offering a model for the development of new perceptions and the expansion of consciousness in the meeting of the necessarily stable and the necessarily changing. The rearrangement says something new, which the individual knowledges would hide, as here, where art theory, atomic theory and interpersonal relationships are complex:

> He leaves under the sign
> 'Café du Dome'
> immediately we are living in a Still-life
> The Painter steps through a gate of bamboo wicker
> a radar pulse at centimetre wavelengths
> strikes her left cheek is
> partially absorbed
> no one attends to its flow's relations
> adjust in due ratio

The room is in the rest frame
manifested by drops on the glass
This is the situation. What happens next
requires our happiness.
Each blink tampers with record of it.

It is not easy for the reader to make this cohere into a single narrative, to reduce it to the fixity of a 'record'. Perception, as Fisher says in 'The Mathematics of Rimbaud', is structured not by the external world, but by the perceiver, and it is 'a structure which can itself be changed'. In other words, as readers enter into the 'participatory invention' of the texts, creating temporary coherences line by line, they are restructuring their perceptions, changing their consciousnesses.

There are, however, elements of a ghostly narrative sensed throughout the texts. There are 'characters' or stereotypes such as the Painter, Photographer, Engineer, Bellman, Informer and others, who perhaps exemplify aspects of divided (or in our time specialised) human consciousness, much as did the archetypes in the longer works of William Blake. Blake himself is yet another character in the project and can be seen, like Fisher, showing his compositional processes: 'Blake crossed out sweet desire, wrote iron wire.' (See Fisher's own similar acts of transformation in *Gravity*; but also most baldly in 'Continuous Innovation 1 – 4' in *Business*.)

A fractal is an irregular action or shape, such as a cloud or a coastline, which is complex, though not now impossible, to measure mathematically and to establish the laws which govern its shaping. Fisher's point in the first part of *Gravity*, 'Brixton Fractals', is that that place in London where he lived through its years of deprivation and riots is traceable by his irregular technique, particularly in 'Birdland' (the titles are from an alphabetical list of dances which have been used to structure the project and bear no thematic relation to the poems). He attempts to delineate the place in sexual, ideological and linguistic terms:

Endless destruction
makes Brixton
Call it the coexistence of prohibitions and
their transgression
Call it carnival and spell out jouissance and horror,
a nexus of life and description, the child's
game and dream plus discourse and spectacle.

In later parts, 'Civic Crime' in particular, the Burglar, who exists outside the society's moral and legal 'prohibitions', yet within its unemployment schemes, 'participates in desire transformed in greed' as he commits crime. Yet this burglary is presented as equivalent to the world of high finance, the other City of London across the river from Brixton. This is a conventional radical viewpoint, but Fisher maps the connections between the forces of capitalism, conservative politics, sexuality and biochemistry:

Everybody is very tired
Earning a fortune

Desire and greed are matched
in a 'she looks beautiful' eugenics
A chain of electro-chemical reactions
summarises into
the will to keep up standards

Fisher's respect for the productive energies of his readers is crucial, as they grasp the opportunities to integrate Fisher's inventions into their own perceptual frameworks, a process which may alter those frameworks. To do so is to participate in a remarkable enterprise which, through techniques that often seem as alienating as modern society itself, actually turns out to be a new complex form of late-twentieth-century realism; it offers imaginative models for constructively engaging that alienation. It urges action, in reading, not passive contemplation.

ROBERT SHEPPARD, 1989

BUSINESS

The sky is not our limit

A perfect fluid where
energy-density equals
pressure and sound-
velocity equals light-
velocity transforms
on the collision of
plane impulsive gravity
into null dust

X-Ray film to X-Ray

Shovel and cloth
or a muffled steel
hits the paving
signals another day
cleaning the summer
garden

'I've Left My Umbrella In A Taxi'

Fuel cracks
horizons over
street–pinks
gun a sound
in deep concrete a
high pitched blue
wheel ticks
weights through
bodies of food beget
hot displeasure fit
anger to uncultivated
din and this defends me

(After Wyatt's Description of a Gun)

The gambler's moll at No. 10

He walks up the alley
catches sunshine information
and heat beneath a hanging
honeysuckle where he scrubs
his body with the leaves
flowers resin and scent
extracts a population
of fleas and walks on

Sweet memories

Puts his finger in his ear
pulls out a rhinoceros
'NO,' the promoter shouts.
'Try it otherwise.'
Puts two hands in his ear
and pulls out a rhinoceros
the size of a pin head.
The milkman climbs onto my shoulder
imitating Tarzan with a grin fix.
'Put it back,' calls the promoter.
'Start again.'

Face scrub

Through what clutched face
sigh   mud   the bridge
better with
shook on the chest

Fish in a bag in
the fridge
letter with
book on the desk

Continuous innovation

I.

Apex socket freighted fought to thrive
New tone dial nine flies free
Window's crack on yet
Set invokes the signal
Waste ground berries
Flips out play executive
Drought ofays may fit
Stouter bright into original speed

2.

A pickpocket rated nought-point-five
Newton's phial nineteen-flies free
Videos interact on net
Setting broke the signal
Wattage ground theories
Sits out play exact
Doubt of ways to say fit
Outer sighting torrid rapide

The only way to get on

3.

A pickpocket rated nought-point-five
Shoe turns while nineteen-o-nine free
Videos into rack on next
Fetching broke the signal
What what down the rebus
Is it shouts Hey is it
Down your weight Hey is it
Out of sight into reap-a-deep

4.

A quick rocket bated wrought alive
Through turnstiles Nighty nighty Three
Videos in the pack on neck
Stretching broke the signal
What what down the road bus
Give it shouts Hey give it
Out of sight into reep-a-deep

GUEST SHOT

As an elephant
I eat cabbages whole
Not interested in the heads of men
their memories loose
in the slough of nervous er
government why
only yesterday capitalised
on the special configuration of food
in membranes the synapse of
a munching process irrespective
of continued molecular turnover
achieved discontinuous recall
of how I got locked
in this cell

(After Francis Crick's letter to *Nature*, 1984, vol. 312, and reply
from R.J. Mayer of Nottingham in *Nature*, 1985, vol. 313.)

Played Against Drum-Beats

Object
ob-ject; noun
as against-the thrown together
as against-assembly
as against-drum-beats

I   FOUR OBJECTS

Photograph of Ganesa idol.
Photograph of Asepsis sterilisation chamber.
Illustration showing iodine rising from a crucible.

2

The inside weight held by serpent-keeper
Siva's son holds the four-beat pattern
Drum, Sword, Bowl & Trident.

Indian Pink & African Pink, both lakes
prepared from yellow, *deserved* earth
Elephant & elephant from ivory dust.

Four-armed, drunken elephant
Pink guardian of privacy, bows
To that moderation, that pity named wisdom.

2/3

Insight moves tending the castle
Ganesa guides the fort father
Cosmic body language.

Perfection
as if the edges were picked out
Wages out of egg dessert and art
Dusk blown in a cloud.

Already prepared to be drowned
Keeping watch in isolation, bends,
within measure, to the invisible.

3

All I move for the a gate
Sight of the keep's well
Emanation of invisible rhyme.

Pink set behind grey-green waves
Signals to the into a closed chamber.
Instruments need not record
Sensual aura multiplication.

3/4

A weight diffused over the Earth's surface
Tyrian power becomes
crusis   crux   cross.

Violet-like vapour
Heating and fusing metallic ores
Diseasing wheat with ear-cockles.

From the ashes of sea-weeds
Pure red & pure blue flow
From the lamp with 4 nozzles.

4

Through an electric spindle Mother makes
The possessors now
Cruise in air.

Iodine breeze
Tempers searching after sources
With difficulty the white-rumped bird

hovers over rock pool

Out of seeds the undergrowth
Unsoiled fish spawn and bright flux
Out of brilliance a nasturtium.

Enclosed Delight

5   THREE OBJECTS

A painting of Erasmus.   A photograph of Alcyone galaxy.
Dürer, self-portrait.   Illustration of the Adam's apple.

Helium in florescent tubes.   Photograph of an elm tree

6   ERASE MUSE

Casting a spell the hands, two sets of four

Dark into a mirror a charging bull
the *prisci theologi* that
'This is my body' denies
'the power of the keys' locked out.

Gold in sea light
yellow to blue embodies
arsenite of copper
and red burnishes trilogy:
a toad.

What price this 'indulgence'
without visibility, magic
and the square root of minus one
boastful of being different from predecessors
rings of iron in blue gold
not freeing nor sound
knot disguising slavery or death.
The laws *are*: but who handles 'em?
too many gates from the city.

6 into 7

This gesting charm catches, suppresses,
keeping the hunter-instinct at bay
Cultured thinking that
Fate renegates.
Green earth
incrusting agates in trap rocks
smeared with sacrificial blood:
appears to make rain.
Who interprets long-suffering value
where understanding becomes algebra,
breaks down imaginary divisions
between spheres, when wand'ring wit
eats its own kind
unanchored in ecumenopolis?

7   GALACTIC ALCYONIUM

Dead men's fingers, clasped
retracted from danger, exhale water
knowing social intelligence can never be free.
From the chest a shining future
and light, reflecting from the Battersea shield
The symbols *become*
relate to fourth thoracic

keeping consciousness in an upward drive.
Celestial flowers
digested in spirits of wine in dark,
a bright sky is without stars;
a naval vessel, into eddies,
leaves after-image, a blue blurr
the 'Kuleshova Phenomenon', perhaps,
a kingfisher
beak parallel to windcock, but
does it quell the storm?
Slow the
cracked open
valve? Is it popping the
vacuum where the
biological loses grip of flexing
moving to airport for take-off?

7 into 8

A conjuror turns symbol to thing.
This is understanding.
Many believe it.
A rocket ascends
Being is ignited, impells toward Necessity
leaving the genetic without correspondence.
The hand and eyes throw dice
for the temperature of a molecule,
for the time to Alcyone.
It is too late to bend the thumb back;   10
There are no hinges, no locks, no brickwork.
Out of self-control
out of reach, thumbs press into fists
too late to recover security,
too late to identify which buttons are dumbies.
On Earth a bushman has identified the flight,
calls it Agni.
Made silent by kisses on cheekbones
he follows wounded prey

through a field of undisturbed antelope.   20
There is no search for City of the Sun;
it remains in his being.
Consciousness of this is High culture, ascending.
On ship a group discuss returns to a Golden Age.
They without food select who is to be eaten.
One has found a key to the buttons;
the throne of choice.
They call him Great One: Seer: Majestica.
His bones are turning to milk.
His eyes are multiplying.   30
His voice is in vapour
and is total control.
His subjects are as sponges. They are too late
to link-in. Too late to sleep to dream.
Their subliminal is conscious.
They devour each other.
It is not another beginning, it is too late.

8   ENCLOSED DELIGHT

Symbol is real sign for the act
transforms understanding the illusion
made silent by belief
that it is physically possible to touch each other.
The forbidden remains in Being,
the shadow follows wounded prey;
a double bind.
Alerted dice rattle, predict pregnancy.
Through a field the weight horny-cells
the neck pulls away from lace, from lapwing-claws.   10
Too late to roll from trees out-of self-control;
stretched limbs pick fruit.
City thumbs press palms
Identity is confirmation, direct recall
frequent pattern repeating known speech, breaking

the throat pips, tree rings in apple.
The hinges hold the door;
energies within aura bounce back stab
of light in stomach
made gnostic given narrative in mouth.   20
Not moving, arms outstretched, an uncoiling serpent
misses hunter who signs his bones too late.
Fruit drops a key, precise kisses on paper;
seeds turn milk from emotion to dream;
day is made painless.
The anchor visible at sea in half-light
compressed subliminal locks compass.
Sponges without conscious brickwork
absorb their own bodies
where accounting itself destroys   30
its own centring in
this the continuous beginning; contraction's push.
The dream overwhelms
absorbed through static skin tossing
control inputs nerves' ends,
transforms, curdling dream spiel,
reiterates namings in unknown languages
chosen by Fate latches
locked unlocked with skeletons
before social conscience impeded freedom.   40
Repetition of culture, grows unifying Being
in City of the body
where one door remains closed.
The symbols not out of touch,
namings chaos pattern,
mis-identities
break Certainty paradigm.
The manipulations from an Outside,
designs continue return
doubt without measurement   50
or statistician's rule.
Darwin's theory disbelieved

came and went in too short a time
to cohere as much as body
rising falling
in thought
without conscious awareness of signals;
it really matches
body-mind
casting the seeds *it* intends.   60

8 into 9

It is too late, to speak of
the state of innocence
where action is indifferent.
Too late to walk naked, to hear
the origins of speech.
Total control is
oppression, heavy metal
compressed, carbon
from tree's rot.
The forbidden fruit stuck   10
in the throat
key to co-operative-hunting
from emotional signs.
Alone, Dürer paints the imaginative garden;
lines and circles at a stroke
without rule without compass.
There is no search for City of the Sun;
fortification has human proportion
followed through
without sketch or altered line;   20
licentious pattern
dissolves colours the
culture that embodies, in vibrations,
objective and subjective
thumb precisely to forefinger,
nucleus unsplit, in self-control;
magistration.

The city with a central gate
where day is known.
A weight of speech measured   30
prominence of perspective thought.
The geneal-tree relating
to Present and Future.
Creation from explosions
dropped where
Belief is understanding
and the symbols are the real.

9   DIAMOND APPLE

The larynx cords, taut,
verbalize the action to
drums beating out free
of subtle learnings.
The uranium splitting
burning out juice that makes yellow
salt of lymph
drain to earth.
The carnation on a faded
hunting-coat, lost
in a pink field
Keep of the castle
supporting mushroom tree
extending grains
to recolour earth
magnetisms
that colour judgements.
The body abstaining from indulgence
in starvation that
breaks pattern
into grids on flat surface
where objects appear as the eye confirms
coloured by a brush in an all-seeing hand.

9 into 10

The nose winces to
winch sense of those who eat with greed.
They may be salt of the earth,
basis of Being.
A red haired sunset and green tunic
against chalk in cliffs.
The treasure-vat of dead bones
hold of energies
without explanation of how
they do not extinguish.
The Adamites answer, looming,
wears thin,
tires us. The meat
of it always suppressed.

10   ALBEIT HARD

But there is more lucrative matter,
halt to the matting
to those worth their wages.
The Math matrix not simple.
Emanations continue make shape
much as they feel free it.
The knot loosened, clenches;
the neck tie. The hidden
food, growing.

Corroding wound
a purple osier ring
on a crab's back;
The shine on lance-head leaves,
on red-twigged willow, may heal.

When energy's source is covered
the knout hardens.
Active care by concentrating hue, may prevent
keeping it to ourselves, without

Spreading by visual language, suppressors

Cleopatra's Sonority

11   IN MEMORY OF ELM TREES

Around spindle springs
grow nitrogenic water in light
ripenings, the treasure
inside vine shedded skin.

From pirouetting
branch tips spin off pyramid fruit
winging air expressing seed's intention
spirallic contraction and expansion.

Respiring out from elm
coriolic elation
light and air stab lance-head leaves
the chlorophyll arrow cues
light to leaf to soil to tree
the wonderful cannons.

11 into 12 and 12   HELIO-CATHEDRAL SONNETS

Molecular patterns, shrinking,
nuclear colonel
out of control, 'hot',
the latent tumour.

Fired generator of water, forms
what Sun will become:
lump of coal, aura in sky yell
owing mist in

vague evidence. Distorted speech:
lake silt over bones and stones,
continue pulsing answers
a matter of faith,
Olduvai as !Kung our

indigo-plant becomes
lilac aroma
first shift of love's emotion
shy and expectant
risking.

Flash clearing air,
pull exceeding push,
life, or Reich calls it bion,
cross-link of breath-colour,

Sun at spectrum edge
fades out, 'cold',
pulsing non-stop pulse
in wrist skin.

Cue bricole; bricoleur
whisking paint.

Gripping the Rail

For Fritz Lang

14   SANDMAN

> Grey graile held
> in eye a glass
> fragment sifting sleep
>
> shafting focus across shields
> against pathos.
> Civilization moving, away from heat;
>
> grey against grey ground
> grizzling sprays
> white and black skies.
>
> Face of astonishment
> a smile of humility;   chromosomes,
> all colours gathered
>
> > this shock of hair
> > the wise cessation of inertia.

13   NECHAEV'S FINGER

> The affair a diamond necklace
> noise of diffused signals
> elixir of immortal youth
> from crystalline stability in antithesis to double helix
> without heart forming a light thread
> life thread fixed repeating
> tulip bulbs form tulips
> perpetual imprisonment.

Deep pity; pure flame; inner self unsoiled;
freemasonry's fortress (San Leone; Peter & Paul;).
From bridled wilfulness
an inner voice calls forth the depths of being.

   The bio–core
   betrays nothing and no one.

15   EISENSTEIN'S INVESTIGATION

Shaft of through a window
light opens a wide-eyed glee,
majesty fingering buttons

shifting prints.
Body bleeding on pavement
receding hair shore

exposure hazard
loss of pain
luke warm violation

torn jacket
flapping newspaper.
In place of labour

   ebullient crucible,
   tension surface changing.

16   HUNTER PLASTICS, WOOLWICH

Trickery, out-pressing work and energy,
injects confusion, plunge, a
moulding retreats, hiss

cools troughing
passion in breath break.
Feed gate clippings control

smelt friction drag of
plastic crates on metal floor
the polypropylene castings and dross without glow.

Observing the enemies of pleasure,
work-complacency moulded
utterly mixing, duplicating movement.

    Self-interfering heat;
    carcinogenic irritation.

17   TEMPLE OF THE MUSES

The hunter instinct
incog, in coded compartments
without blurr without decency
static thinking
attracting dust

Imaginary picture of
  a wounded antelope
crossing Heathrow airport.

Ancient plaited sandal; Englishman's brogue;
Arab woman's slipper; steel-tipped 'safety' boot.

'Study of clouds'.

    meditation.

      Study of particles exposing
      particles. Limitless skies.

18   FOR MAUREEN O'SULLIVAN

From lens a screened
a bronzed body
in ceremonial cloth;

businessman with Bryl–Cremed crown.
Tense muscles the four knuckled fist captures
instinct, cultured shading
beneath high rise, eye shadow.

Sweet dreams
adding machines
Saturday-morning flicks;

a char dusting elsewhere
polished rubber plants a table

    torn photograph of Clark
    maybe Errol Flynn.

19   'THE PEACEABLE KINGDOM'

Tethered cow in body
the created city
circle of bone
proclaiming fierce sap breaking through

a lilac flower
pushing out from shade

Brompton Stock, or it is Sea Rocket
under St Margaret's Bay cliff, set back

avoiding another brain
change another civility

harmony and peace with the animal kingdom –
cleansing's death.

Strip off, go swimming,
conceptualise count-down.

20   15 OBJECTS IN TWO SETS

Etching of Count Alexander Cagliostro with
     brief biography.
Photograph of Mikhail Bakunin and a letter
     from Bakunin to Ogarev November 2, 1872.
Drawing of injection moulding construction.
Map of the Americas showing distribution of
     Indian tribes.
Drawing of boot types 'through the ages'.
Photographs of busts depicting Homer, Hesiod,
     Solon, Sophocles, Euripides, Socrates,
     Plato and Aristotle.
Painting by John Constable, 'Study of Clouds'.
Painting by Edward Hicks, 'The Peaceable Kingdom'.

Photograph of leg wear forms.
Photographs of Albert Einstein, one with
     Marie Curie.
Photograph of Sergei Mikhailovich Eisenstein
     and a clip from his film 'Ivan the Terrible'.
Photograph of fingerprint index at CID
     headquarters.
Clip from the film 'Tarzan the Ape Man', starring
     Johnny Weissmuller.

Clasp Flow Other

Clasping the neck this
affair horizon chain of crystals
Unreachable railway
carriages repeating
dream Flow through belly through
fortress in fear to open all
Gates, eyes signal motion,
grip vision behind screen
Migrating metal, cloud
flowing hold, back watching
Wisdom never indifferent
to push out to grip it
Hold ungripped
flow charge the changing
To control the
filling graveyard body pity.
Machinery man
fractured making aware that much
pink Crystal stability
hazing eye pond skid
Light moving flow through
(
Allows the measurement
geometrically, coldly bombed.

    That much grip firm
    you can feel silence nothingness the
    Animals plants too tied untired
    to itch this need to be Other

THE MATHEMATICS
3   OF RIMBAUD

After art resolutions made earlier this century the idea of art as objects and poetry as poems gradually lost credibility. Since then many attentions of activity have emerged that, initially through conceptions of art and poetry as process, and as idea-oriented, began to rethink what they were. Continually in the process of formulation, but already an essentially regenerational and multivarious complex of fields, the new works no longer find taboo in the object, but include objects and processes, process-showings and methodologies in a world of multiple possibilities that is giving, at least to a small attending audience, a vital cultural necessity complementing the political arena, without being its voice, and without grounding in theories that, for instance, *Art-Language* fixed upon. It is a requirement of this art that, to answer Olson's 1962 'A Later Note on Letter No. 15' (page 79 in *Maximus II*), the poetry is always 'yet to be found' in the process of its making, and that making continues to take place through the physiology of the reader.

Simultaneous with art and poetry's disillusions with traditional practices came a multiple crisis in the tropologies – ways of perceiving and interpreting ourselves and the world. Before the turn of the century (and in too much mainstream art and poetry this century) the tropos had been made inside of neo-Platonic resolutions. In the early eighteenth century Leibniz, and many subsequent generations of morals, ethics and poetics, saw literature and the human mind as having a consistent quality – as being able to offer in their essence – elements that are stable, against which judgement may be gauged and which will remain of value across history. That 'we act in like manner as animals, in so far as the sequence of our perceptions is determined by the law of memory . . . I assume it as admitted that every created being . . . is subject to change, and indeed that this change is continuous in each . . . if there was no resemblance of what one had been, immortality would not be at all desirable . . . this immortality which is desired includes memory'. The tropologies in his *The Monadology* (1714) and his *Discourse on Metaphysics* (1710) consistently suggest that 'we have in our minds all those forms for all periods of time because the mind at every moment expresses all its future thoughts and already thinks confusedly of all of that which it will ever think distinctly'.

Korzybski, in his *Science and Sanity* (1933), offered a different tropos in saying that, 'Perhaps neurologically, animals *feel* similarly as we do about "time", but they have no neuro-biological means to elaborate linguistic and extra-neural means which alone allow us to extend and summarise the manifold experience of many generations (time-binding). They cannot pass from "time" to "times". Obviously, if we do not, we then renounce our human characteristics, and copy animals in our evaluating processes, a practice which must be harmful.'

To accept Korzybski's tropos, on initial consideration, may appear to dispute Saussure's assertion that analogy is a reno-vating and conservatory force[1], in as much as it uses old material for its innovations (see his *Course in General Linguistics*, 1915).

It is here that René Thom's particular clarifications in his *Structural Stability and Morphogenesis* (1972) come into sight. He makes clear how the mutually necessary manifestations of continuity (or structural stability), are linked to the leaps made possible by this spring of the already present. It is a coupling of the *relatively* slow dynamic of consciousness and mental activity to the simultaneously multiple rapidities of the auxiliary systems (physiological and otherwise) and the outside environment.

---

[1] The English translator of Ferdinand de Saussure's *Course in General Linguistics* translates the French *conservatrice* as conservative, which may make ambiguous the sense given in the French, (see notes 11 and 14).

It is part of the understanding of human perception that whilst the same object can exist in many different guises, it may still be recognised. This is the classical problem of concept clarified by the Gestalt psychologists. If you solve such a problem by naive intuition you give to outside things an existence independent of perception and understanding.[2] Understanding acts as a transformer from naive intuition to informed intuition – it includes the difference between what Chomsky, and earlier Lenneberg, gave as innate, or biologically based, language and the transformations of that language by living. We may think of this as consistent memory coupled by inventive memory.[3,4]

Joe crossed the road this morning for the third time using the same number of steps. He hadn't been interrupted. He wasn't even consciously using the same route of the same number of steps. He hadn't thought about it. Had he counted the steps he would have been aware of his consistency. Even so – he may not have been so obsessive about discontinuous change as to deliberately vary the number of steps, or to change his route in order to be unable to walk the same number of steps each time he crossed the road.

It becomes necessary to recognize the probability that the properties of connections, reversibility and indecompossibility which define the space of the same object (i.e. the structural integrity of the Gestalt) have as origin not the physical properties of the outside world but the constraints of the dynamic of our structure, a structure which can itself be changed.

---

[2] Thom notes, 'The most convinced solipsist, when living and going about his (sic) business, must adjust to the world outside and admit its structural invariance in his use of it; does this not amount to admitting the existence of a certain reality?'

[3] Noam Chomsky's essay 'On the Biological Basis of Language Capacities' in *Rules and Representations* (1980).

[4] Eric H. Lenneberg's *Biological Foundations of Language* (1967), used by Chomsky.

It has been demonstrated that experiment and measurement, irreversibly disturb the evolutions of most, if not all, processes. But the process of Poetry, to the extent that it is successful, is not simply experiment or measurement, geometry or arithmetics. There is no stability of a larger number of events. So that, whilst there is no intelligible language without a geometry (or underlying dynamic whose structurally stable states are formalised by the language), it is also clear that as soon as a formal model is intelligible (admits semantic realisation where a meaning is apparent), that intelligibility changes in relation to the meaning another may give it, or in relation to living after the first realisation of the intelligibility. And the meaning may take on a multiplicity that is summated or left incompossible and so forth. Saussure made this clear enough in showing how the interdependent parts of language function and acquire value through their relationship to the whole.

In 1937 Andronov and Pontryagin in the USSR[5] introduced into mathematical analysis the idea of structural stability. Their concern was a qualitative study of differential systems. They saw dynamical systems as structurally stable if a sufficiently small perturbation of the field did not alter the qualitative nature of the system. This does not require that the homeomorphism commute with time; the perturbed system may have a completely different structure from the original system after sufficient time has passed. That does not change the description to unstable. The growth of bones can be considered a structurally stable system. The early Greeks' contradiction-in-things can now be stated differently as a stability, or consistent turbulence I will call *Thesmos*, made to turbulate inconsistently by the moral and renewable law of *Nomos*. But that's not enough. Poetry has a stranger charm which presents, when it is successful, a transformation of love and language, that is informed by the laws of *Thesmos* and *Nomos*, the consistent and the invented, in the realm of preter-memory known as the imagination.

5 A. Andronov and L. Pontryagin, *Systèmes grossiers*, quoted by Thom.

However, there seems to be a time scale in most natural processes beyond which structural stability and calculability become incompatible. In planetary mechanics this scale is of such an extent that the incompatibility is not evident, whereas in quantum mechanics it is so short that the incompatibility is immediately felt, and, for the present anyway, the physicist sacrifices structural stability for computability.

To look again at these matters: Heraclitus (more than 2,000 years ago) saw all morphogenesis as the result of a struggle. Easiness from such simplicity (the statements are of course fragments in any case) immediately carries complication. The simply beautiful morning conceals the complexity of perception – blaster cattled. The simplest examples of 'struggle' – the junction/bifurcations used by the nineteenth-century Riemann-Hugoniot mathematics – specify the topological structure of local shock waves, but the only existing universal model for their case occurs in gradient dynamics from previously known polarised domains. Homeostasis, by the demands of living, becomes a stability that requires, for instance, negative feedback to maintain momentum. Nature tends to blur and fluctuate transitional regions under the effect of viscosity and diffusion, an Einsteinian collage, the yellow syrup pulsing in the pavement as Joe crosses the sunlight are the cracks full of yellowing moss glistening in thawed frost; the moss fits to the crevices, is discontinuously retrodden. Poetry is not a flower ascending through that moss, but a made steel mobile tripping the walker. The movement is made possible not by the thermodynamics (initially) but by viscosity and the irregular diffusion of differently sized parts. The overview conceals the particulars. An overview of biological systems defines membranes as separating two systems, and a particular attention can show a membrane to be a system connecting two systems. A similar case can be found in the description of vortex streets in hydrodynamics in the theory of wakes.[6,7]

---

[6] Refer J. Z. Young's *Programmes of the Brain* (1978).

[7] Refer T. R. Oke's *Boundary Layer Climates* (1978).

In contradiction to Whitehead's view that 'we cannot hope to be able to discern the laws of nature to be necessary'[8], Waddington's chreods – the idea of change inside *necessary* paths – begin to offer a better contribution to a contemporary tropos.[9] Waddington differs from the more general overview of the morphogenetic field in the privileged role allotted to time and its orientation. Irreversibility of time is justified by the fact that, for natural processes which depend on diffusion and are, at least partially, controlled by parabolic equations, the possibility of qualitatively restructuring the past from the present situation (retrodiction) is much more restricted than that of prediction. Dreams become easier to comprehend than histories.

If a process studied is contained in a unique chreod, such as in the finite language Husserl calls for in his *Origin of Geometry* (1936), or the single completely resolved form of every expression discussed by Wittgenstein in his *Philosophical Investigations* (1953, written 1926–49) (Wittgenstein of course also allows for things which cannot be said in factual propositions, but which can be shown), or the requirement intrinsic in the *Answers for my Critics* given by B. F. Skinner (1973)[10], it is deterministic and structurally stable.

But Waddington's concern with chreods is of a different order. He uses its description to show that biological order is otherwise, is, for example, epigenetic – gradually producing and organising – rather than predeterminedly genetic and singular. Information theory, for instance, is unable to specify the phenotype's rules of formation. A matter Chomsky's generative grammar interfaces.

It seems likely that some conservative[11] natural phenomena

---

[8] A. N. Whitehead's *Science and the Modern World* (1925).

[9] C. H. Waddington's *Tools for Thought* (1977).

[10] Skinner's answers appear in *Beyond the Punitive Society*.

[11] The English translator of René Thom's work remarks that he has translated the French *economique* as conservative.

give geometrically imposed realisations of these privileged dynamics; this is a possible reason for the presence of internal symmetry groups in the theory of elementary particles.[12] But spaces with a natural measure having a macro-symmetry are few and are mainly limited to crystallography.

It is generally supposed that classical mechanics deals with phenomena of the macroscopic world, which are therefore rigidly deterministic, whereas phenomena at the quantum level are fundamentally indeterministic. But these views carry faults, in so far as the former may be uncarefully applied to social science, and in that the latter's argument – the uncertainty principle – is based on the crude and inadequate model of a particle as a point (however accurate some of the qualities of that principle are). Certainly, 'It is the theory which decides what we can observe.'[13] In the macroscopic world of a universal differential system parameterising all the states of the universe, any such model can be subject to experimental control only under the conditions that the model has a localisation procedure allowing the construction of structurally stable, local models.

Now it is everyday experience that many common phenomena are unstable and there are no experimental criteria to distinguish between a structurally unstable process and a fundamentally indeterminate process. The question of determinism, freed from its philosophical background, reduces in phenomenological terms to the almost incontestable assertion that there are phenomena that are more or less deterministic. The degree to which a process is deterministic is essentially in the expression of the degree of smoothness (differentiability) of the evolution of the process in terms of its initial conditions. The degree to which a process is determinate is determined by the local state of the process. This is not a matter of calculable

[12] Refer Gerald L. Wick's *Elementary Particles* (1972).

[13] Albert Einstein in conversation with Heisenberg, see *Physics and Beyond: Encounters and Conversations* (1963).

prediction, as so many generations of morals, ethics and poetries appear to suggest. The determinism is one of quality rather than quantity.

Look, I've got an electric calculator, the cartoon character says. Ask it anything, come on anything. Will it rain tomorrow? The calculator is plugged in, the operator looks up, replies: It may. If it does it will be wet.

So in any process there may be regions that are well determined and structurally stable, being Waddington's chreods – the canals of consistent memory – and instabilities or indeterminisms – the generalised, unformalisable changing topologies – the poetries of the inventive memory; and these processes are the concerns I wish to elaborate on in arriving at the informed memory that brings about not the consistency and conservatism[14] of automatism, but the informed intuition which is the becoming of the mathematics of Rimbaud, and the multiplicity of attentions that has continued to ensue.

---

[14] The usage here refers to the wish, not to change, but to preserve and fix.

2. acuity.

The problem of assessing, or agreeing to what is in focus
continues. The singularity narrowed in a region of spacetime.
Detail resolution, acuity or sharpness, in the difficult of a
fixity. They've tried contrast as a parameter of vision rather
than luminance. They've tried repeating a pattern giving
thresholds to measure contrast sensitivity function with
relative phase.

The range of difficulty moves from finding spatial resolution
of peripheral vision, through Fourier analysis testing vision
with sine wave grating patterns, into considering information
in parallel channels. With the exception of written characters,
we need to recognise most objects over a range of visual
angles. There's no simple way to be sure that the image seen
down the scope, or in a photograph, corresponds closely
to any reality. Using a variety of different preparation
techniques, many feel reasonably sure that the structures they
observe exist. But Heisenberg's qualifications persist. The
photographer working with Hanes at the Anglo–Australian
Observatory explained how he massaged the plates to obtain
his images, and then added 'representational colours'. In
special cases a technique called kneading has been used to
improve the synthesis–radio–telescope maps significantly.

The idea of coincident signals in different frequency
channels begins to provide a framing device, but work on
electrochemistry, matters of conditioning, coupled with the

human variety of sensitivity, has a long way to go before
acuity can be a term clearly applied. Matters of memory
and perception also persist. Vygotsky finds that, according
to Edward Sapir, 'the world of experience must be greatly
simplified and generalised before it can be translated into
symbols. Only in this way does communication become
possible, for the individual's experience resides only in
her (/his) own consciousness and is, strictly speaking, not
communicable'. But alternatives to understanding, and to
focus, ensue.

Example: Any finite value can be attributed to Doppler
velocity shifts, gravitational shifts and instrumental effects. A
physical event is inseparable from the measuring instrument
or the organ of sense that perceived it. In studying solar
oscillations, the observed ratio can be made using alternating
measurements of the intensities at the relative positions of
the solar and laboratory lines. Conversion to the equivalent
Doppler velocity involves adding the line of sight component
due to the Earth's orbital motion to the Earth's spin rotation
to the shifts due to gravitational potential, added to the
possible time-dependent instrumental effects and the signal
due to the solar surface oscillations.

Work in *Gravity/shape* also considers the complex of
interpolation in human spatial vision, the perception of the
upright, and of colour.

21.   magnetofield. magnetodynamic.
magnetohydrodynamic.

In an experiment to find alternative generators of electricity
I subjected a high velocity flame to a strong magnetic field.
Declared attempts to paint the weather. The electrons then
constituted a current flowing between two electrodes in a
flame.

A simple, perfect fluid flows through spacetime. It might be
the Earth's atmosphere circulating in the Earth's gravitational
field. It might be interstellar gas accreting onto a black hole.
Whatever, or wherever, the fluid may be, its motion will be
governed by the curved spacetime laws of thermodynamics,
plus the local law of energy-momentum conservation.

Magnetodynamics is the result of magnetostatics plus
covariance. The structure looks like a collapsed egg-crate.

Magnetohydrodynamics considers the motion of an
electrically conducting fluid in the presence of the
magnetofield.

The magnetosphere (Van Allen belt) is pulled in over the
Poles, and is thinned out to form, roughly, doughnut rings
around the Earth. Some of the magnetic force lines move out
of the cusp at the Poles where they clash with gravity. That
is against the solar wind pressure. They are stopped short at
the edge of the magnetosphere – at the magnetopause. The
subsequent looping is incomplete – neutralised.

Magnetic windows are susceptible to solar penetration and
allow exploration of correlations between the sun spot activity
distorting the magnetosphere, and the magnetic field's effect
on the weather.

Example: The average level of geomagnetic activity increases
3–6 days after the disappearance of large solar filaments.

25. non-harmonic oscillator.

John Berger, 'Perspective makes the single eye the centre of the visible world. Everything converges on to the eye as to the vanishing point of infinity . . .' But there's not agreement about the latter.

Art-Language, 'It may be that some people thought that perspective was *the* means of representing reality, etc., but no one thought that buildings actually vanished. Perspective was a projection, like map-making. The competing methods in map-making (Mercator vs. Sinusoidal projections) are not liable to make claims as to which is appearance and which is reality . . .'

Oscillator waveforms can be broadly classified into one of two types – the sinusoidal, or harmonic: and the nonsinusoidal, or non-harmonic. Non-harmonic oscillators are also called *relaxation oscillators.*

Example: 'Separation is itself part of the unity of the world, of the global social praxis split into image and reality . . .' DeBord.

With the generalised separation of the worker and her (or his) products, every view of accomplished activity, and all direct personal communications among producers are lost.

30. pin-cushion.

A kind of curvilinear distortion where edges that would
normally be recognised as being straight (say the top of a
picture plane, or a writing table) are curved. The distortion
can occur towards the sun, where the outer portions of
an image are seen from a stopped-down simple lens. A
rectangular picture plane can be seen to resemble the shape
of a pin-cushion or pillow. A similar effect, say, partially
obtained from some selenium copier machines, when taking
a copy from the middle of a thick book, where horizontal
typeset lines take on the curve of the page made by the
spine's binding. The lens effect of the universe, that is where
gravity can focus light to produce two or more images.
Example: The quasar discovered in 1979 was first thought
to be two. The illusion is created by an intervening galaxy
acting as a gravitational lens.

Pin-hole distortion refers to defects in gesso panels often
due to over-dilute glue solution. Pin-holes were made by
renaissance painters to transfer charcoal drawings onto primed
canvas planes by pricking the charcoal lines onto the planes.

32. plasma.

Mineral science refers to a bright green, translucent variety
of cryptocrystalline silica, chalcedony, as plasma. Electronics
gives it as a synonym for the positive column in a gas
discharge where there's no resultant charge (the number
of anions and cations is the same). It is a source of radio
emission. Physiology refers to plasma as the watery fluid in
which blood cells are suspended. Cosmologists still speak
of a primordial plasma prior to galaxy formation and soup
ambiplasma. Note also, plasmolysis and plasmodesmata in
plant physiology.

In 1958, Hubble's ex-student, Allen Sandage, discovered
during research into this area that what Hubble had identified
in distant galaxies as bright stars were clumps of hot stars
surrounded by a plasma ionised by stars. He consequently
became involved in upping Hubble's distance scale. Vid.
Sandage's notes on the use of a jiggle camera smearing images
by moving the plate in a rectangle during exposure.

Painters, and some sculptors, refer to moulding the substance
in their work. Plasma occurs in thermonuclear reactions like
the sun. The social amoeba, *Dictyostelium discoidem*, cell's
sudden action release of cyclic AMP in many ways resembles
the sudden active inrush of sodium ions through nerve cell's
plasma membrane.

33. plasmapause.

The occurrence of large-scale plasma convection within the
Earth's magnetosphere, driven by the external flow of the
solar wind, has long been recognised as being of fundamental
significance in determining the properties, structure and
dynamics of magnetospheric plasma populations. There
continues to be controversy over the kind of physical
processes which couple the magnetosphere to the external
shocked solar wind (magnetosheath) and which initiate the
convection cycle by transporting plasma and magnetic flux
from the dayside boundary into the geomagnetic tail. The
two main possibilities have been a viscous-like interaction
associated with wave-particle interactions and plasma
diffusion, and magnetic reconnection between the wind and
the flux. The two processes may coexist.

Jones' Antarctic Survey remote-sensed the plasmapause
in 1981. It provides a *source* of natural radio emission.
Radio noise is observed by spacecraft in the plasmatrough
(the cavity of low-density plasma between the Earth's
plasmasphere and the Earth's magnetosheath). Escaping
non-thermal radio continuum (overlapping so that it
appears continuous) can be thought of as distinct beams of
radiation, with different frequencies from different regions
of the plasmapause, and not continuum at all. After multiple
reflections the beams from numerous sources are scattered and
merge to produce the radio continuum.

35. quasar.

After a dinner & dance at the first Texas symposium on
relativistic astrophysics in 1963, came the discovery of
quasars: the very distant, compact objects emitting large
fluxes of light and radio waves.

At one point it was understood that quasars embraced any
galactic nucleus showing evidence of non-stellar activity.
In 1963 they were interpreted as powerful examples of
gravitational collapse.

It is *expected* that there's some way for the central regions of
a quasar to *remember* a particular direction, for the lifetime
(sic) of a quasar as radio source, say more than a few million
years. Variability of radio emissions (frequency or intensity)
from most quasars is plausibly attributed to radiation
emitted by relativistic electrons gyrating on magnetostatic
fields. Imagine acceleration from a vast synchroton.
Imagine the universe's expansion as part of a 'rhythmic'
expansion/contraction pulsing ions into a maelström brought
on by spatial distortion of the bioplasma. In this connection
correlation among Hans Hofmann's concern where,
Expansion and contraction in a simultaneous existence is a
characteristic of space: Wilhelm Reich's hypothesis where,
The biological direction 'toward the world' represented
in expansion, and the opposite direction 'away from the
world', . . . represented in contraction, seemed to me to
have a primitive model in the mechanical act of expansion
of a pig's bladder. Note for instance, the streaming of
cytoplasm in fungi-translocation of nutrients mixed with such
rhythmic/oscillatory matters as the malonic acid reaction dealt
with by Winfree, bringing a myriad subterranean into the
reality of a sonatina.

Most quasar power appears as either infrared or ultraviolet wavelengths (human eyes see between these). The ultraviolet flux is probably responsible for photoionisation of emission-line regions from which red shifts are obtained, and hence the distances to quasars. In many, the bulk of the emergent power may even be in hard X-Rays (where hardness is the degree of capability when moving through matter opaque to light).

Supermassive, black holes at the centres of galaxies have been postulated as a possible explanation for the quasars and other active galaxies. Some have suggested they may have condensed out of primordial plasma, prior to galaxy formation, or this is a time trap derived from linguistic static.

Various authors have attempted to invoke white holes as explanations for quasars, oblivious, apparently, to their perceptive conditioning. The white hole hypothesis is thermodynamically unsatisfactory: that is, physically improbable. Hawking suggests that, because of quantum-mechanical effects, black and white holes may be regarded as physically indistinguishable. Penrose, however, considers this, and continues into showing that they don't physically exist. The white hole hypothesis may be fun, but like making a sestina after researching hermeneutics, attraction ain't all there is to eloquence.

Abramowicz and Nobili report two main theoretical models for the central engine of quasars, and other active galactic nuclei: the black hole model and the spinar model. They note that, whilst observations of the time scales of flux variations *can* rule out the black hole model, the accretion disk theory shows shorter periodicities as consistent with it.

43. singularity.

Unless the Earth's surface, or a picture plane, is made as at least two disjoint regions there *always* arise points, or curved paths, at which the distortion is *infinite*, vanishing. These are called singularities, that is where the rate of change of one variable with another exceeds all bounds, and where a big change in an observable is caused by an arbitrarily small change in something else.

Example: In terms of variables whose physical import is immediate: spacetime singularities associated with black holes and the heat capacity that ushered in the quantum mechanics of crystal lattices under the description 'ultraviolet catastrophes'.

Warning 1: singularity as homonym where it can simply mean a point where something singular happens. In *Ideas*, as in catastrophe practice, a different space is involved, the space of control parameters like loads on a structure, or tactile boundaries like the edges of a picture plane, at which the configuration of equilibria (singularities in the engineer's sense) or at which pigments meet independently (as in Hofmann's later work, such as *The Clash*, 1964, *In the Wake of the Hurricane*, 1960, or *Bald Eagle*, 1960) in time, undergoes change. (The Hofmann paintings are in Berkeley Museum, a catalogue is due out in spring next year (1983).)

Warning 2: Kenneth Wilson suggests avoiding infinities altogether by working with fields that have an underlying lattice structure and which (in the case he studied) are then incapable of giving rise to ultraviolet catastrophes. (In lattice gauge theory, inherent arbitrariness of an Ising lattice problem in thermodynamics mirrors the arbitrary gauge of the electromagnetic field.)

Back from the diversion, on Earth-ground, singularities are avoided, they are zeros in the core of a tornado after the wind velocity falls. Colour mixtures vanish into greys. Rhythm gets flat, or becomes zigzag without fundamental-frequency as a component. The mathematics involved checks with Yung-Chen Lu, Zeeman, Poston, and Thom.

In addition there are phase singularities, which, in an abstract sense, are those that involve no rhythms in space, or in time, but only irregularity in mapping a disk to a ring. The inevitable discontinuity turns into the most localised and violating kind.

47. *Subsequent Looping.*

1. Subjective
    states formalise claim universal
        assent
    the, blocked emergence
    from a
    condition of irrelevance
    question now
    the constant tool reducing to the
    common denominator of a mere
    celebration of the senses' frame

2. Nothing left a shared destitution
        rivered
    ignored the significance of conduct
        as it relates
    to intent
    self satisfaction
    behave like a billiard ball directed
        at a pocket
    damper to revolutionary
    directionless joy

3. Radio window
    simply what is grasped
    discover concrete transactions hidden
        behind the mechanical
    image of reflection historically
        specific record

4. What could
    have collective rug pulled
    nearly torn beneath
    a held taut banner the possible

5.   Lost all
     that could have for pleasure
     honed into
     special cases whose forms are
     inextricably cojoined in their
          cultural context
     each search for
     renewal made research rationalised
          inside personal autograph
     alternatively many responses
     carefully interfaced gradual change
          of the muscle tone with language

6.   Exploration and making bring
          unpredictable perceptions invented
     to address someone in the risk of
          destroying or
     gather fragrance sound
          respiring new tissue

50.   torus (toroid.)

In electrical engineering it is a coil or transformer
corresponding to the shape of an anchor ring, contributing to
entropy generation. Bill Griffith's *Zippy the Pinhead* enquires,
'Excuse me . . . are we serving donuts in another solar
system?'

Ion-supported tori are included in the discussion on radio jets.

One dialectic for analysing electron waves and acoustic
waves in solids and electromagnetic waves in space, uses a
3-torus shift. I made one from a rolled and glued copy of *The
Financial Times*. It disintegrates Euclidean stasis.

Toroid is a doughnut-shaped mould of a scour pit, made in
firm water sediments by an eddy or whirlpool in flowing
waters.

Example: One two-dimensional mixture of a ring is the
surface of a doughnut. A surface that can be found by
swinging a ring around in a ring perpendicular to its plane,
that is, the product of two rings. The topological space of
a ring might be the phase of an alternating current, or the
colour of a lizard.

Andromeda viewed by radio telescope is the such of a
distorted doughnut.

55. Zig Zag

Regarding the retardation of radiation and other aspects of
entropy and the question of source-free or sink-free radiation,
Penrose discusses singularity and time-asymmetry. He uses
a stone thrown into a pond as the start of his notion. Later,
he considers an alternative hypothesis, continuing extensions
of window, where a stone is suddenly ejected from a pond,
accompanied by ripples propagating outwards towards the
bank. (I had used a topographical analysis of a breaking
window and a graph of circadian rhythms in Winfree as the
plan of the poem *Bending Windows*.) The phenomena was
shown in my film *Kessingland*. The idea is close to the culture
dreamed of, where, rather than seeing the zag motion of
an infalling stone's propagation of ripples, the waves are
ziglike. That suggests the 'probable zigzags of the revolution'
(MacDiarmid) and the pleated sheet in hair, formed from the
zigzag shape of keratin structure, accrete from the *zickzack*,
the jagged edge that dodges about.

Banda

Took chances in London traffic
where the culture breaks
tone colours burn from exhaustion
emphasised by wind,
looking ahead for sudden tail lights
a vehicle changes
lanes into your path and birds,
over the rail bridge, seem purple.
A mathematician at the turn of the century
works out invariant notions in a garden
every so often climbs a bike,
makes a figure of eight around
rose beds to help concentration,
then returns to the blackboard.
The schemers dreamed a finite language
where innocence became post experiential
believing the measurable, ultra-violet from a lamp,
isolated sunlight curvature
made false language what can be done
to separate
from perception.
In a dream apparently without volition
a car burning and
watch myself there
sealed-in beneath a smog dome
uncertain what to try for next.

Midnight: a solo of the Nightingale. Great silence.
Open a gate
against hinged pressure of rust,
white pigment to denote reflected light.
Singularity burgled up the drain pipe,
a busy rush pursued tenderness at its slats
padlocked into pastoral quicksilver.
'If one of my students should one day rear children
in a better way
Surround myself in music, that is physically
forget the dream as a move towards preventing
objectification of vision.
Legal power, completion, smothering,
on the shelf flashpowder and a can.
Practice to assist improvisation
holds onto the pattern of railings
a super-structure of sound–curve symmetry
recognised, and examined, by autodidacts.
A bunch of type in my palm
populates fixed compartments.

Exasperation from a lack of clarity
sighs towards singular objectives
trapped into them
without realising
the peripheral fleets
glanced at knowingly
as an indefinite refusal
of euphony,
or until the variety gets coded
into an analytic container
dropped from a winch onto the quay
When the road shifted
one part lowered
then pushed out a halting arm
over the ridge
carrying a reflex camera
to record the wonderful.

A recollection of a hill so far from London
I burnt lying
in a dream for thirty minutes
and woke in a grove of oranges
smelling of eucalyptus.
The up and down different to anyone
gravity
or opposes anthropologists of science.
It took six minutes for the exercise
and the lot was cordonned off,
Water Lane
to Brixton Oval,
our future in the air
over the walkway busted polystyrene
scattered,
a sonata for piano and jetplane,
coöperatively struct,
now a mount of cars piled behind a subsiding dyke.

4 A.M. the Hedge Sparrow, shriek of the Hoopoe,
the Song Thrush on trumpet,
a large ball rolls by
hits the sentry box
and the road opens.
On one side a ley line buckles
into the wall of 'The George',
in the machine a solenoid blows
a rush of green vans and police weapons
send the needles into peak
and damage the Dolby.
Your freckles expand and you blush,
a black clock and two batteries,
my fingers tingle to let the blood back
we roll over
temporal inversions or points of view
burn the air,

and memory, slatted into alternations,
begins to rely on the instrument panel
as well as the force
felt in the chest
as speaker loudness increases.
The explanation of the universe gets
considered as shared awareness and truth
a bucket with a hole in it slops suds over
the top of a tiled floor
until we switch it off.

Two electricity lines,
three gas mains,
carry enough energy across the walkway
for two sets of loudspeakers
face each other across the
dancing
visitors at an island of science
see the primitives at work
describe the utility of pilot lights.
The furniture in the room appears to be stationary.
I am half sick of shadows
under pressure of personal feelings
a poet crushes a carton marked 'Shredded Wheat'
in a corn field,
calls it a poem.
Laid out on the lawn
exhausted
the burden of personality lost
in untimed contemplation
independent of unified law
uses signs for other
than what they signify
by filling navel with powder
and exhaling a cough.
I suppose it is in me and coming out.
The quantum leap

between some lines
so wide
it hurts.

The shelf falls from the balcony
shatters,
erupted aluminium silicon
scratches airliner windows.
Two water mains, three petrol pipelines,
a large sewer
in the walkway,
where a tree has broken paving,
build a fire
and get the kettle started.
'The fact is,
when ole bill came along,
we brassed him up.'
You know, all I wanted was to recover
without retrenching.
The pipes don't appear to be busted
Just keep it open
I'll go down and see if it comes through.
Telephone wires, and a mile of new road
cross purchased fields
Listen to the echo
of wings' fizz
before we get to them
and resistance
in the reduction to utility
and functions.
Fraught, but underneath it
resistance without armour
as if that were possible,
following a wire stretched across the page
until pen drops off the right edge,
and face
the red background

in the morning
noting where it came forward
in front of a glass bottle
to restate the four-colour problem
broke it there by facing it
The yellow and black road bar
lifts to an angle congruent
to the prison roof.
Bird carpets in the hay
wood. Noon:
great silence
haywire.

Began to decide how to perceive
Dreamed once of where we were going
too precise about direction
said, That's the way to the city, but
I wouldn't start from here, if
I were you
knowing what could be meant in the clang shack
bolted upright
just before the bell came
steel wheels on steel rails
run through the lounge.
It's the city alright
felt in the tropai of directions
the joy and worry in a traveller's back
back from market with vegetables
incapable of doing harm
Leaning the bar into a distribution curve
at the chicken jerk chally
across from the betting shop
or as if based on notions of we have
been here before
or another says that makes such a perfect match
you could use 'em as bookends.
Carried the system down Coldharbour

on the right shoulder
two circular speakers
plate the inner ear just
passing through
your living space
moving with a deliberation
seldom found in poetry.
It happens quickly not as you might expect
takes a long time moving towards
its suddenness and when it does quicken
it surprises. Even so, as I say it,
it has gone and a more deliberate
or expected mode takes form,
changing the minimally real at once into
a memory
chequered in a rebound
cage labelled 'Development'
an unattended box of timed light
marked 'Don't Touch' or Volume Control'
as a measure of decay patterns
the Bellman recedes down the walkway
catches my eye
with a Brasso glint
carries a refrigerator on his back
shouting 'Ayeyay'
until someone, I think it was Edna,
calls with a camera, 'Hey boy, here!'
Gradually I predict the possible physically
and the probabilities that this
will occur. I stand in the walkway
with tracts on good and bad
tearing them
at once excited by the energy
of doing so and recall
the situation
brings the distance involved alive.

Silence: Brutal punctuation of morning:
a Warbler explodes for the last time
an intuitive doubt
passes through the window
regarding the rest mass of photons
at once discarded
at zero.
Enthusiasm sighs
and fear forms in each lachrymal valley.
Blake leans back from his window
down onto the page
eyes partially blind from flowing
writes vigorously across the faces
drawn there, saying
the tear is an intellectual thing,
crossing it out
knowing the trial pended
and anger disrupts thought
momentarily
in a cloud shift, his wrath
blazes reciprocally
stands at his door looking out
into a bright day break
the sirens have stopped
in the near distance a blue spark
leaves the prison roof
an inescapable sadness, thought of
as reflections onto the window
call it condensation
the glass breaks.
I get a dust pan and brush.
The light lengthens and the
utility of cleaning up
sends a shiver into me
it must be getting winter
I begin to cry quietly inside
the strengthening chill

of alternations
Carvings of flowers on a sword blade
catch the spark
I thought I had imagined
then realised
the sword was polyethylene
and the kid hadn't
taken off the tag
spelling out the price of it all.

There was some dancing
but what's really going down
in this male age praised by noodles
an innocent obsession with turning lecterns
coded in digits.
A firelighter in a screwtop can.
The Fireman calls in for the situation report
concentrated in depth of an advance
The unliquidated resistance remains
blank-screened in the blast.
Yesterday I met a man who wasn't a misogynist
felt a necessity
to move into a new mode of life.
The sun energises autonomous
care with weather
and anamnesis
breaks a trend of cut-off
through history. But what else goes,

It is a lovely morning
light adds shadows
The Fireman's report abends the actual
spins in the sky frame
turn from the strictly utile
for aid duplexed
with how things were once better
over the hill

The freedom to act socially now
measured on a breadboard.
Bike boys come down the walkway
rear their burners
almost together on back wheels
at entrance to a workers' council.
She takes a torch into dark room
and light pencils scratches onto the box
circumvents the mechanical
description.
Swept me off my feet,
A policy of time
in a carpet factory operated by
each person each free
moment the space to stretch.
Scratch marks when the pen ran out of ink
still on the manuscript
something potent resides on its validity
unbroken
tradition but
let's actually find out, you and I,
what that can become
with another
arrangement.
I atomise a liquid into my hand
from my breath
it adheres into an uneven smudge
read as it changes colour
the background moves
through it
selectively imprints a warmth.
Thought it might be self-love
flattered by envy until
she saw a different hand there
crumble soil around a new catalpa
a folded sign posted to it,
what it means to forget what has past.

A range of sprays from the lid
sweetens the casserole
He added another pepper then chopped in some basil
The sign unfurled as my head touched
the pillow
spread my perception to speak.

The Bellman and Fireman meet at 'The Windmill'
exchange notes on salvage.
They are who they are
yet remind me of what has gone.
She bathes in rain water at last clean
for the first time in decades
A sign calls me backwards
'Beware. Society Ruled By Men'
The urge to destroy is not only a creative urge,
in the distance a man sings
accompanied by his own hands and feet it
brings sighs of enjoyment.
An apple stew secretes into it,
smells of cinnamon, cloves and nutmeg.
I rub my cells in them
coaxed by such overwhelms I somersault into a grocer's
a flurry of wings crosses the enlarger box as it flashes
three balls hit the railings complex
the sounds.
If the rebuilt city is resistant
it opens to those who strengthens it welcomes
the travellers on the ways to themselves
Now where are we . . .
I cut open an apple and its wasp goes
hesitant body line made clearer by holding
the sound of skate boards and rollers
launch from a ramp and the joy
wet zings say it as wasps
fed from our bodies surround in changes of light
a dog in the other distance

It was as if the subject itself lost materiality
Bird carpets copied get copied
Value, meaning, determination repeat.
For fun she snaps a photo of the Bellman's cart,
reality and notions of poetic stress merge
simply doing more than two acts at once I cover
the bottom of a warmed pot with Assam.

Disturbing this silence
two chaffinches on two violins
in a biological lock watch
fixed by light chemistry in the eye.
The call of 'Let me out,' becomes a jig
along a cordon of police,
values from others, opinions, and
deliberately propelled into distance correction.
I am almost what I wish to live.
Outside in the walkway three kids play on wheels
One expects more respects for prospects
includes a desire to manage
A figure of eight with a müller to
slurry tempera on the glass.

Around the World

This gravitational song meted against displacement
The slow movement of holding you
By the lake, deep amid fir and silver poplar
Dream sleep's energetic function
During meditation each finger rayed in cactus spikes
Blake crossed out sweet desire, wrote iron wire
It was the discovery of human electromagnetism
made a sign, opened curtains, revealed the garden
Mouth perpendicular to mouth energised desire

All the weight and attraction that limits movement
A Mercury mix that replaces theft with eloquence
in the face of visitors' astonishment, experienced veritable bliss
A robust memory in the flares of lost and added synapses
So that the vines burst from my fingers

In the space of shape-time
We move our fingers and simultaneity becomes falsity
Sheltered by wall and hedge
Translucent superimposition several distinctions one
synapse   And the garden becomes geodesic for a moment
An *imitation tomb among the vegetables*

A mango tree under a dull cloth, stirs its tentacles
A rush of calcium through my nostrils

That the complex is Nature's climate.

Passed out in the dole queue from an overdose of guerillas
satellite bang.   satellite bang.   hits the
negation of morning confidence and hope

Took a stopwatch into her mouth and spat
Reduces premiums to the political, to the sentence , ,
'and the simple at a discount

'the imitation stage has been passed
In a blue self-portrait the background continues the face
a gigantic plane tree
Given a part, consistent memory appropriates a whole
Flicks mercury in a meter   rolls off a glove

    Dealt out cards, silver-foiled dinners and cans
    piece. pease. pierce. sleight of hand
    Friendship as virtue an inventive memory combines
    varieties of inconsistent features
    Take my hand, the silken tackle
    Stored associations of the cellular net
    Swell with the touches of flower-soft fingers
    Rode shaking from the park on flat tyres.

claim of pastoral confidentiality
The return to copying pre-empted by cultivation
its enormous trunk
The net's avoidance of overload and too much overlap
Take this palm to your mouth and fill it with grapes
A Net of Golden twine   many synapses
Semblance of worth, not substance
spawn of an entire lack of interest, but some surprise
The return to cultivation pre-empted by synthesis

enter, stage right, 'the creative centre of civilisation'
pieces of granite, broken and numbered, rejoined with cement
Its mighty branching and its equilibrium
Hard-wired to compensate against malnutrition and toxic
waste   The danger of important words
In tears clothed, in dream sleep's shed, avoid obsession
Humane Eyes over a blasted heath
hand holding a book, first finger inserted to hold position
piled granite on the lawn like an enormous potato

Imagination sown meter again then this place beat
In search of ways to reverse-learn junk city
the gravity of its preponderant boughs
Sighs damp down potentially parasitic memories
Mother and child constitutes a society
reservation or rather reticent in flak of rhetoric
Enterprises based on innocence   a pleasant sufficiency
Creative imprecision to emphasise flux of meaning

    A future bright blocked by bricoles.

Strapped own earth underfoot to walk base without trespass
Took for exercise of virtue
O sprinkling the garden, to enliven the green!
Dream's random noise shorts-out unproductive activities
Ran out of faces so stopped action in film
A degree of benign limitation
Flummox then repose your wearied exercise

    The gravity occasions gone petered against retrenchment
    A hard task in truth I attempt
    In my garden   face lift   modifying spine shape
    Reverse-learning to modify cortex energetically
    Floral dress hung from sculptured timber
    Intellectual innocence in a pretence to value
    Play area scattered bricks painting garden
    Then the perceptions begin to repeat
    The garden that should have bloomed once

Doubled oscillation preludes another chaos
Confidence beyond consciousness
And do not forget the shrubs
Dream's selection to enhance retention
public elects pinball physics
In the face of wonder experienced a kind of vertigo
Trapped in a cage then allowed to sing.

'Responsibility for the present state of the world
The terror of feeling that consciousness may be
functional   Where are the sentiments of my heart

Simply kissing, with you on the balcony
Into a world not entirely song
Lifted all the baskets   *Even those without berries*
'the Paneubiotic Synthesis
muscle   neuronal excitability   energy generation

to complete harmony laid biggest lime full length in garden
The constantly actualised, shuddered chagrin
In the garden nothing but evergreens
Ungratified desire reminated each moment
Short silence followed by a thud.

Ballin' the Jack

1.

Compassion fatigue –
three loud whistles in quick succession
following a bright flash
hit head on foot bridge.
The strongest trees may survive
width of the flushing band,
a telephone fitted in the garden
on a poolside desk rubber plants.
A doily folded in his belt:
, bulb spot sixty watts, olive oil, honey,
functionally improved recall after sleep.
A moving bang came through the window
modulates permeability across blood-brain barrier
What is it?
a sucrose intake of less than 12 spoons a day.
Sequacious breed reactor
another Take; melodic sweetness; on the prison roof;
indifferent to any importance of verbs
lunch-room physics applied to international relations.
Rain balls
the deconstruction of hope
a varied pattern of bangs experienced as waves:
erasure.
Continuous finger piano
wires over a plane
body colour over pencil with surface scratches
bale out soon.
Equalisation of accessibility beyond private taboo
topological dependence of plasma membrane.
The propellor larger than this flat
at the hub   delusion; greed; hatred;
painted green.

2.

Painted blue
a couple in the yab-yum position
an umbrella spread with my knees flat.
Tropical independence of miasma frame
a muscular energy available to many:
dice gripped then thrown.
At a drive-in, set in curve of railway, an aircraft.
We had to cross the river on a two wire span.
Chopping waves
a dynamic construction
brightly painted fences.
In a given place, to say precisely what demanded
dances, with straps,
learnt from the physique requires interpersonal relativity
different from the posture of surdity;
strengthens muscles of the heart and rectum.
Sequentious freed enacter
three dessert-spoons of fibre offered as minimum breakfast
'What's that?'
modern relations of permanence cross-out with indefinities.
An orangutan can throw in chaff snow
punctuates proven records with leaps:
, work light, ironing board, oligotoil, laundry,
adroit fingers in his impact
on the pool table stretching, potting.
Even with keys to 'phones we cross the wires at night,
one for your feet, the other for hands
strung through trees without insulation.
In the walkway a wig stand
rolling a bright flash
I could see the head in total darkness
a tiredness from exposure.

3.

Wired-up from explosion
didn't know until flash fired
what I had captured.
In the walkabout a mercantile stance
electric fence protecting track from slides
two tiers of chains.
Evening breezes weird moss, fires our sight.
A petal table stretching from the pot
dried fingers rub the thermostat.
, light work, bored ironing, olitory oil, money,
pumiced grooves and traces of hoping
meringues snowed in icing sugar.
Monolithic relations permutated across life lines.
Question identity and gender
enough salt from sufficient fresh produce
extremes of brevity; a history of joy; on the prism root;
preserved in the smack of reflections.
Indignant to the appearance of birds
built on the bowers of paradise
in the garden in front of a work hut
a mossy lawn with objects grouped by colour.
Standard configurations in coördinate transforms
noble lies
Ah, Wilderness! self-improvement anxiety,
on site of a torn sapling a twelve-year-old log.
A sharing of joy and sorrow
cleansed in acidic rain
a continued search for terminal Nature
the vegetable enemy of novelty.
Wung in poverty
an idea of feeling and perceiving the day
in grey ink, Beneath the white thorn lovely May.

4.

Parallelograms overlap his back's muscles
reopen a discussion of limits and vanishing ratios.
She crossed burnt grass to the windmill
over scaffolding and beneath it
read graffiti on play wall where
two kids work sand on dead lichen.
Everywhere homeless everywhere home
heads of watermelon and wood carved from same plant.
Travel literature; works of sex; life on mars;
a dreamer led out of confinement into servitude
works out relativistic perceptions, faints.
With a wad of bark she paints bower with fruit and charcoal
reorients work hut into a constant direction
expels a spitting intruder and repaints green with liverwort
jammed in the kiss of remembering
wears badge of lost innocence.
Activates presence by continual renewal
Questions each movement, each renewal.
In a Brixton queue stopped for lack of identification
harangues slowed through a tannoy
Hands worn hard with broom handling,
scrub pavement, paint railings, polish steps,
dread fingers dub in laundromat.
A lily pond stagnant from dead bacteria,
even freezes, bone welts, frost mires, her plight
two tears of rain.
Fenced in, a society without engagement
now the walkway a gang with clubs
sirens rising falling.
O my Lover and my Friend,
a future blight brocade.

African Boog

Went dicing on my bike
>Disappearance
>Meaning given by timbre
>Relational invariants from a flux
>She lives in advance of her days
>>Speed
Rooks carry aubergines over Tulse Hill station
>He hung an 18 foot blackboard in the garden
>In all the beautiful continuity of hope
>>The innocent
She crossed Hillside Road with her sun lamp
>Thought confused by recall
>A car in flames
>>IN the climate
>Distress of need
>Moments when the go different two-beat series
>These are birds is an illusion
>>Confront
>Down the escalator that ascends
>Constituents of multiplicity unaffected by transformation
>Pauses, and, introspections
>>Their own terror
From his mouth produced a net curtain the length of his body
>'Surrendered myself to magic, that is physics.'
>Watching myself burning from a distance
>>Spectacle it unleashes
>Authority, perfection, oppression
>Moments when series go different the two-beat
>Improvises from consistent memory
>>Violent in itself
>Her attitude's beyond music called indirection
>Configurational relativity, the sound of language
Dissing on my skate board
>>Population
>Your patience is exhausted with someone

'To catch a fly on the moon'
The default of the garden's charm
    Each other
Hooks vary auburn jeans overt until fashion
    Discontinuous strata, unsteady sediments
    Closes behind her the gate of childishness
      Always ends up
All the oranges, but one, turned blue
    Tripped up by details
    Down Electric Avenue in a garbage press
      In future war
    Overlapping fourths with thirds
    Essential and accidental property.
    The sound of the heard and the played
      With dirty hands
'How to count the stars while riding a bike'
Moments when go different the two-beat series
There are birds singing
    Deterrence
Cycling into seeds and mud
Relativity on the flip of invariance.
Autonomous order disorder
    Truly violent
Juxtapose time a-cross-rhythm
Your forehead blur-laps beneath mustard field
Two moments when the two-beat series coincide
    Only the turn
A metal box in flames
Constructed proof for consistency
In perpetual *leans* accelerates
    Against the military
Fools about contemporary with falling
Topological correspondences unfold similar linguistics
    together.
Extemporise from inventive memory
    Superversive
The *shapes* of the figures 2 and 3 make music

Loved to dance
She enters the enchanted garden
    Because insoluble
At the velocity of milk in a vacuum flask
The rough edges, the false starts.
Just pumping up my tyres
    The spectacular
In opening amazement a tulip stretched beyond return
A misdirected intensity of discovery itself
That this isn't universal experience
    Simulation
She's lost in a mode with a fun loop
    Stratigraphical completeness sifted in differences
    Expectations may be high
        And appear suddenly
Foam, issued-out produce, a certain learning commodity
    Spans far longer than experience
    Just warming the pot
        Terrorists, public opinion
A direct hit on the waste basket
Undecidable
In a purple lean-to, accumulates
    System which
Walking down the drain and laughing
Contextual and stylistic alteration
Buckled beneath a fruit stall crying
    The stupidity
Counterpoint reduced to fracture two and three beats
'Tables, chairs, and beer mugs'
Spontaneity from electro-chemical decision
    To exterminate joy
Juxtapose pitch notes melody
Disappears in bluebells   wood-light   may.
Moments when the two-beat series go different
    Actuality can be the meant
Absorb myself by watching
'He looked so *innocent*'

Crouched in a doorway mumbling
>   To palm all that is reported
Juxtapose harmony-notes vertically chords
Every turn within change;   joy and worry
Just ratatouille on the gas
>   Innocence
Brixton market frequent, Brixton market full music
At odds with results from everyday
Just imagining pleasure
>   MAKES all the variables
Tempered by the moon on his shoulders
Instead of feedback through the eye as a basis.
Perhaps an uncommon or personal experience
>   A minimally real event
Orangutans guessed, but one yearned it was true
Few study deposits for as long as a decade
Its shades slow with promise
>   Flashing
The chair left through the window
>   The proposition without deduction from other
>   propositions
>   Play drum with the drums being heard
>   In a maximal echo chamber
Two moments when series coincide the two-beat
'The laws of nature's independence from the choice of
>   mollusc.'
Tigers are in cages, tigers are in cages
>   The contradiction in situ
The mud of perfection
Relations that have a finite ideal
Just come in
>   Does utopia
With joy and fear small thoughts at large
The process being followed conceptual and executive
>   together
Skyline in the window

Patterns how many years
A civilisation based on dancing
Assumptions on visual evidence reduced to syntax
A mix of two-beat moments invigorates texture
To open for measuring time
Flames
This volume determined by the size of needle
Just smiling as you
The personal alters consciousness
Shape of your eyes' dilations condense brights
The particulars of each plant heightened by common
structures.
Absorbing the memories chemically
Changes
Two moments two-beat series coincide when the
Stars detail variability shows an average everywhere the
same
Horizon into the window, the siren
Initiates
Older parallels and pseudo-parallels overlap
'Tomorrow we went to the forest'
Just playing in the mud
To think about a problem publicly
Shone from a helicopter onto a tulip
The rug rolled away
More often than not reprevented
Political to value slowness
At viscosity of spilt ink vacant tasks
Stratas record positive deposits, but what else happened?
Blowing metal into tumblers of cells
Had taken the possible
JUST ICE
Immediacy at the thresholds structures activity, that is
perceptions
From the balcony over the tulips, the church

The society made by men
Juxtapose timbre vibrato to patterns vertically and
    horizontally
Opens a glow-out red jacket in a crowd.
Asleep in a hammock, accelerates
        Dance collaged into reel
Conversation and your breath bell
'It happened that I found myself tomorrow'
Four playing cards on a box in a crowd
        Implosive order abolishes
A language based on tone and timbre
'No one will drive us out of this paradise'
Seduction turns to exploitation
        System of repression
Her stare reft thought in a winder
Span's illusion independent of the probable.
Stolen wallets on a bread crate in a crowd
        The order of transgression
Indiginer and invader overlap
'It was tomorrow'
Space toys on a pavement in a crowd
        The old bacteria of law and cultured intrusion
Speech patterned horizontally and vertically
'Ya! Ya! Ya!'
Or enchantment becomes repression
        Value, meaning, determination
Asbestos beauty snapped in a rain storm
Reality a requirement for perfection
The sound of memory-played with memory-being-absorbed.
        Excess of rarity
Two moments series coincide when the two-beat
Without limits, the universe of these beings is finite.
A street in havoc, exasperates authority
        Law, point of view, evidence
Lifts from a spring board into cloud
'Temporal separation a tenacious illusion'
Every turn of the path seductions

Entrenching the desires of others
As best as you can rapped from the brain bourne
Jump on bike, figure of eight around rose beds, to the
blackboard.

Bel Air

At last it octobers, a tremendous
mist descends on my head
trip a cat
an obo hits my incisor
I fall back
'Good Morning, this is the News'
Is this naiveté or integrity —
this simpleness or confidence to gaze
with intelligent vitality with
numerosity a
splendid buzz from a razor that,
spaced out on a slowed down recording,
reveals a fluff in the magnetic arrangement.
This is Europe
it's not even a terminal.
Forget arrangement. Stop.
Replace with manipulation. Stop.
'Thankyou, but this gets us no where.'
A Burglar near the end of the century
looks out over his balcony
and reinterprets the State,
Everything now appears to take place outside
Work's quantum determines the permanence of violent conditions.
Of course he's sick of it!

Shall we follow?
He leaves under the sign
'Café du Dôme'
immediately we are living in a Still-life
The Painter steps through a gate of bamboo wicker
a radar pulse at centimetre wavelengths
strikes her left cheek is
partially absorbed
no one attends to its flow's relations
adjust in due ratio

The room is in the rest frame
manifested by drops on the glass
This is the situation. What happens next
requires our happiness.
Each blink tampers with record of it.

2.

Shielded by these particles autumn
offers astonishment.
Instead of organised hatred she
involved in disorderly performance
made necessary by the floods
weaponed through the fence
an entourage of western medicine and humiliation.
She paints at the gate
the struggle of objects for supremacy
The Burglar crosses a room and knocks on
my eyes, He touches my mouth
with the edge of his trembling,
He frames me with my own perception
as it internalises.
A yellow glow seeps past the door
he leaves open
The community buy dogs
to protect him.
Boys argue furiously over
their video systems
The Burglar sells his watch.
The Hamming code suggests
a drop–dead halt.
They are calls for a clean-looking page.

The Painter moves from the gate
persuaded to contain impatience
through unexpected calm and firmness.
Lamentation and grief become the patterned

stable world, make guests of those
who belonged.
She matches the found pattern
of a star map
into a knitted pullover without
a look forward to the outcome except
a knowing of its warmth
recognised through texture
It lifted the debate of production
and autonomy out of the Burglar's
bag still wrapped
in newsprint
and opened it out.

3.

The children recognise the cloud shapes a
mathematician codes as corank one.
They see the dynamics
without knowing the internal parameters
and one girl trailing the drop-offs from
a running toy
turns to her now stationary vehicle,
'We better go inside before it rains.'
The Burglar leans out of someone's window,
lowers a box of sand
onto the walkway. He
is insecured by men and scraps of paper
permitting him to live.
The Painter follows a path to a simple hut.
In the wet an umbrella loses its
commodity function. She
rejects this. Professionalism's
insistence incites her anger.
I am tired of the news
and play through a contemporary
Quartet at twice its intended speed,

swapping one note for another
then dropping loud breaks of sound
mid-rhythm into my weakness
leave my initial appetency
for another weave.
The reflected radar pulse
returns through the window with a
second. The star map begins to craze.

There is talk suddenly of mortice locks,
with another, hasp and staple,
inside an alarm sounds
from a car in the road
we know, beforehand, we are in a city
We call this knowledge but
are also in out of place
no room to move without limits
The Burglar rings a bell for help
It is a mistake
We are alarmed and our
vibration changes colour
randomly our rhythm chocks
and my breath catches hers.
She leaves a half ounce of casein
to soak along side the alcohol
and ammonium carbonate
It is enough to fix the image
made of the Burglar
She continues to walk away from us
up the path to the hut
without identity, carrying
a torn drawing marked 'Studies
for the engraving: Adam and Eve'.

4.

A reader follows the marks up the path
occasionally losing balance from
may be
synaesthesia
stopped short by the figure
of Blake, kicking away sand and pebbles,
joining the path
naked beneath his raincoat,
locks my eyes.
I imagine he has just been
writing a tract on astrology
'Irrational action,' the Painter notes,
'From rational self-preservation.'
I respond to the stimuli realised
as alien to my experience.
The mathematician adds a calculation
through spurious adaption to realistic needs
This paternal acre is a colony a
usurped matrilocality
'The stars,' Blake could have added, 'Advise,'
mitigating fear of the inexorability
of social processes you create
as reader.
The Burglar moves that
everything negative
is due to the outside
A flight of birds,
released to tell the time,
superimposes heat patterns on the star map.

This creates a spatial illusion
One colour appears above the other
through its transparency.
What may have been noise
gets read as fresh knowledge.

It carries understanding that the
collective distribution of virtual utterances
creates the social set-up the
institutions breeding
value judgements about innate tendencies
or irreversible actions.
The Burglar moves over another barrier
behind the window
unaware a camera
records this onto film.

5.

It becomes apparent from the film
a dance is underway
The Painter moves towards the open
hut. The path has muddied
before her from heavy boots
and the overlapping tracks
of a bicycle. It creates an
apprehension which increases her
exaltation gives it momentum.
She stops on a stone to sustain
deep breaths and
reels from them.
The smell of elm bark accentuates
this. Women like her participate
in the war against coöption.
What she creates prevents subjugation
by the State, but it is no longer possible
to point out exactly
how.
Yelping dogs remain quite distinct
from bird life. Yet some of
the sand she threw at her painting
remained there, became gems there,
what blew back from the throw

took some of the slurry from the path.
She enters the hut to find she is
there with three others. They sit in silence
smiling.
A loud bang moves through them,
followed by a draught.
They all rise and walk down a
second path. She begins to
question this. Her palms are itching.
A playback is underway on a wall
with accentuated wood grain.
The silhouettes of the viewers
interfere with this, but
clearly there is no figure on the
display. They watch a window open
and net curtains lift. They see drops
of rain move across the floor. A
chair lifts from the corner and
moves through the window. There is
a sound of shovelling. Everyone
begins to get the creeps. Their laughter
ceases. A box of sand shuffles
across the floor to the window.
'Stop it!'
The Painter turns to the others,
they are asleep and lean over themselves.
The smell and colours moving in the
room complex. This pink noise
becomes an image
set before her.
'Stop it!'
She turns to the others but is now asleep.
The Burglar switches off the playback
and moves to the window.
It is raining. Its breeze
turns a wooden toy on the play box.

'What's going on?' the Painter asks.
Their coldness astonishes her.
In such a set-up of standardisation and
threatening sameness, she is positively
cathected. Their silence becomes
the voice of an estranged society.
The pattern of the star map at her feet
has settled into a streamlined adjustment.
What it now tells her is useless.
In the walkway a man carries pavings on a
trolley to the sanded mud and begins
to lay them down.
I lay back on a pillow to feel his
movements recorded by the light on the ceiling
and the sound of his ram.
The loose bricks, old frame, and some
discarded footwear, form a heap in the walkway.
'It's over the top,' the Painter said,
'It alienates the reader.'
There is an emptiness
measured in proportions.
Democracy is given a high rating
on the opinion poll. She takes down
a bottle marked 'Pure Water'
from the shelf,
'Shall we fuck first?'

6.

'Anyone else want to ring the bell?'
the conductor asks.
I cross the city road to the walkway.
On the slab a scraped block of ox-gall
to break the tension
The Painter is in the garden
following a thrush.
Children are roller skating with

a ball on new paving.
I lift a tract from the shelf
and weigh it. No physical
entity escapes this surveillance.
It frees all concern about issues
of internal consciousness — violent
motions, unknown forces, tortuously
curved, even multiply-connected
geometry. Dealing with a point
simply makes contradiction. This
swarming, the mathematician
calls multiplicity. 'It's a
matter of intensities,' the Painter adds,
'And velocities and temperatures and
decomposable distances,
'You have to use your
intelligent body
to *feel* it.' So much needs to be done
to know the consequence of shape.

Birdland

1. An image of the Engineer's model
    shudders in a basement
    as sand stabilisers are loaded.
    The left arm bright gold, the ears glow green.
    Out of its head energy spatialises
    overlappings of spiralic fields.
    A figure appears to attempt flight,
    it may have wings, yet held to the floor
    accelerates towards an openness through liberation
    of its partner, unseen from the pit entrance.
    Is it male? What is there to say
    concerning child birth?
    Its presence takes place
    between table and pasture, at this moment
    takes space between road and underground river:
    it is named jouissance:
    The arrival.
    It brings experience of radical separation of self,
    like child birth, produces an object of love.

2. In the morning television I carry
    a cylinder of heat in my embrace
    down a garden path labelled by the placing of stones,
    Hey Bellman, someone shouts,
    puts a match to a felled lime
    lengthways in the walkway
    with meanderings of drama
    thought I was moving forward
    lost ground
    in mistakes, with grinding gaps in what I know about
    fidelities or reproduction. By chance, it seemed,
    back to the path I had opened
    Its trace visible in footmarks and
    potential infinity to an unknown fold.
    On certain days, this morning is an example,

I remove my helmet cross the path
with a slight intoxication
to check the lime has been properly extinguished.

Endless destruction
makes Brixton
Call it the coexistence of prohibitions and
their transgression
Call it carnival and spell out jouissance and horror,
a nexus of life and description, the child's
game and dream plus discourse and spectacle.
On the edge
of death High Road, the Busker
starts up a reel, it begins as dance interlaced
with anger. I guess at the ridiculous partners
that perform. The busker dances with
her saxophone
'Ideas of Good and Evil' are subsumed into this nexus,
production knots and
unknots paranoia
Blake stands his ground
on the Common asks, Are
    Her knees and elbows only
        glewed together.

3.   A woman came down the walkway
     lost in transport
     exploded her language at a kid
     with a stick
     restrained by another who breaks
     the rod across his leg,
     We've had enough, got it! We've had enough!
     One hour later someone has dragged
     a felled lime onto the walkway
     Its leaves make a green path
     A pack of dogs surround this, yelp
     out of phase. Down the High Road

a new siren on a police weapon
fills the walkway
It leaves a burnt fizz overhead
grooves the mud plane on the roof.
Next door fits an extension to his aerial
changes tone of CB interference
in loudspeakers makes audible
amplified pulses from a geranium
in a Faraday cage. A poster snaps the letterbox.
Come to Paradise in Brixton's Coldharbour.

4. Beneath helicopters
Brixton abandoned
challenges the closure of meaning
so far removed, nothing will have taken place but the place,
flattened housing for ecological reasons,
fuses with a beyond, a successive clashes in
formations, memories of bodily contact, but
warmth and nourishment do not underlie the air.
The Mathematician
gets on the subway in a pinstriped
with a microchip blackboard. A spotted handkerchief
matches his tie. On the back of his head someone
has singed a domino it
matches his ear rings. As he starts to leave
his accounts, he pulls the arms from his jacket,
sets them alight.
The effect is laughter,
an imprint of an archaic moment, a threshold of
spatiality as well as sublimation.
Suddenly a path clears Sleep relates the squeezed
State to a lack of community He leans
towards me, Last night, he insists,
I had a strange dream.

5. The imaginary takes over from laughter,
    it is a joy without words, a riant spaciousness
    become temporal.
    The demonstrative points to an enunciation,
    it is a complex shifter straddling the fold of
    naming it, and the autonomy of the subject.
    Wearing four tones of grey soap I
    read photocopied pages on lighting effects,
    the Mathematician battery-shaves and makes
    notes on squeezed light using a notation
    echoed by remnants of beard clung to hydrogen
    on his trousers. Subjection to meaning gets
    replaced with morphology. I become a mere
    phenomenal actualisation moved through a burning gap.
    The irrational State insists on control.

One poem from BUZZARDS
AND BEES

Buzzard Glide

Early in morning staple
snapped the defences
Hysteresis as a function
of the Burglar's constitution
relates his transgressions
across public and private
There's something about the
initial state of her appearance, her
arrival, that embodies the memory of
recent past just as the pattern
of magnetisation gives a clue to
local repositories of events
to be smeared out
by the extreme conditions
of her arrival in his perception.
Specified variations in his DNA
led to differences in his
felt experience; wavelengths differed
according to the protein component in his
rod and cone cells
The photopigment embedded in the infolded
membrane of his receptors, initiated electrical signals
from absorbed light
His nerves find the ratio of
quantum catches in different classes of cone and
regenerate images of the past
His mimesis thus prescriptive

rather than imitative
Concerned with those constitutional deletions
which overlap a cluster of separate but closely
linked genes that pattern the development of
the kidney, iris, and urogenital tract.

In one example, the Burglar took
skin fibroblasts from a householder which he fused
with hamster cells using polyethylene glycol
and selected hybrid clones
in an atmosphere supplemented in the garden
by fetal calf serum and ouabain.
These hybrid colonies were expanded and
recloned through the mains water
experienced eventually in both general,
and in details, as toxic rainfall.

He looks up to see the figure again, to
assess the pattern of its arrangement,
to recognise it.
His inhibition as he does this partly
enhances the tuning of
his orientations.
Knowing where he is encourages knowing what it
is that confronts him.
She sees him as apparitor and bawd;
as if from nowhere
yet here to exploit her.
Beekeeper with emphasis on returns;
on the idea of feed her sugar, then
smoke her out.

She drops a tract on late triassic
tetrapod distributions
revised according to per-taxon extinction rates
punch-carded against
the paeleomagnetic signal carried

by thermo-remnant rocks.
The Burglar locks in his data regarding
chromosome 11 halotypes determined by
the segregation of restriction alleles in
somatic cell hybrids.
Mass extinction may represent a significant
departure from the background rates,
but it events in equally timed space.

Reflecting on the obscurity
of this image the Burglar begins an
analysis of his judgement
and its relation to interpretation;
the discrimination of the physical
parameters of each transience
What in the fleeting was hard
to count, harder still to
replicate, because of an absence
evident without tactile sensation.
To put it differently
the conditional probability
that what he saw existed
relied on his confidence.
In order to analyse and thus
orient by patterns of polaroid skylight
all he needed was an array
of receptors, a template, to
scan and match the patterns
in the cosmos.

All the while I feel my fit
my joy stand upside down for it.
And still the farther off from her
Dear Sight I am, the readier
As she emerges from the frottage she
projects that which sees itself in him
from the patterns in the spat-on wall.

Break-a-Leg

Yet somehow a mocking Clown without personality
fastens onto any activity that catches the
face a tourist's movie camera
The shows alternate plimsol and walking boot
In one hand a cane the other a rattle

The aim of the research
to compare the spatial characteristics
of position sensitivity to awareness of movement

Four planets stretch out to the right
of the sun in the morning sky
We landed on the opportunity after Noon
without dependence on time perception or our emotions
Without weight
There were stonewheat thins with Montery Jack cheese
south of the jet stream

To speak of the moon as an opportunity
unleashes the ghost of its presence
and colonises the speaker
underdevelops civilian economy

I take out my pollution handbook
to hear the news and start counting
The rate of beats decrease
as we descend
into a lower temperature and question the biochemical clock
Calcium carbonate drips onto a peak of stalagmite

In transport with therapeutic seating and minimal ploughing
without jellybean repeats
the competition melts
The manufacturer's input of Faith *and* Money
creates confidence
burning tumbleweed on the edge of Interstate 25
Says, Unleash the leopard I stand astride,
This is VCR time
Here we crash cars before they are built
for people that don't yet exist

At 9000 feet with 120 air speed
radar and lasers probe our structures
west of Alamogordo
without Go-Star's navigational alternatives
to commercial radio and ground control registers
we locate   a kink in a pipeline
Later follow it across the Los Pinos
mountains to the drop zone
At 8000 feet the land is remade 3000 feet below
scrub, roads and housing become
lichen, petroglyphs and pictographs of habitation
Geological lines crossed by animal tracks
Paths of nomads following geology until
break natural formations,
leech alkali, hang ristras, then move and leave
Animal   Sun   and Water signs pecked into desert varnish
alternate rods of snail mucous and graffiti
'Gean I can't get no feed,
I can't wait for you, April 1st 1930'

We need preparation time
the proper frame of mind
to ensure effectiveness
A photographic alignment of the land and its image
creates synchronicity
Lifting in a cabbage crate or simply walking
at 7000 feet
haematite and
lizards spiked on barbed wire

As time passed the clock descended the winder-rod
and shadows lengthened
Men of iron with syrup ropes moved downslope towards
rock alligators and blue bushes
soapweed   pinyon   juniper   and sagebush   alternate coded
speech in a glottal cough
In shock control I listen through ear sponges
on the gas-phone to an inversion tube on the horizon
'We're at point 14 diverting traffic there;
 We haven't got anywhere to put anymore at the moment;
 Is your cordon in?
 All buses are to be stacked;
 Over.'

A generation of controlled crashes and fly swats
puts an X on the end of the runway
Digital clock time
Clasts of sandstone and sideritic ironstone
form surface alluvium
Mass wasting in a downslope gravity
partly conceals coal interfingering marine rock
a periodic transgression and regression of the sea
and filth winds.
We circle the house
and the occupants waken and feed us
But don't touch fingers on meeting
On the ground in Real time a pinyon drips a stain onto

tarmac   It is the only moisture for fifteen miles
Snow geese form another horizon in the binoculars
A Yagi boosts the end-fire receiver and
a voice repeats, 'The Range is hot,' from the missile site
The place becomes a cinema
The effect of tourist speed on landscape
An aesthetics of disappearance
a dromoscopy in which we no longer reflect

Black lava fixes its flow before white sands
In a hologram of a human skull 2 million years old
a leopard's canines have penetrated the cranium
dragged its kill out of reach of hyenas
This excites the rattle trap of mythology
preserved in paint by a Blockhead
transformed in film for analysis
the plague of intelligence

The research notes cabbage patch dolls;
a spinning cow on loco-weed; and
greasewood burning on the range

Sinking into a cavern more than 700 feet
takes 3 thousand years
Clothing goes yellow in floods
of damp and moth iced visitors
I look out into successive perspectives
The sun sets and rises in a single window at once
Pink sand, yellow cake, broomweed and meadow larks
contrast reading the instrument panel
at 4 inches of mercury suction
We hit turbulence
Any divertissement loses grasp
Subliminal comfort multiples quickens consciousness
a vivacious reflection
to guard off a conditioned crack.

2.

With the need to lock into personality I
hit a button on the whack box to
start the dirt talking, Here
it comes now
start the talking, Here it
comes to nothing in the essence
trap, Comes to
needing
abandon
Take me, Says,
Clean the limescale on the structure
and take me to
my seed, Say,
Let's get rooty in the
wet house
electric burn in the wet
house.

From a Deptford balcony
an aerial ascends
at 70 degrees,
Below it a fishing-net.
The only occupied
flat in the block,
three shot guns in the
lounge; derelict buildings
all over London.

A vertical system transforms horizontally
where identity is ambiguous by a two-choice
smiz. Plural identities form
a variety of vociferations informed
by transformed systematics and
the Clown steps out
starts eating from the trash-can.

The Re-Destruction of the vertical stripe
and horizontal band, the Re-Dissolution of line
and edge, the Re-Obliteration of texture, the
Re-Abrogation of asymmetry, the Re-Demolition
of shape . . .

Arm locked on a glue bag to the railings
wards off blossoming in Water Lane
Leather belted to the extremity of a thunder clap
to mitigate the fatigue from wandering
under the spread
It broke out like a rash after the experiment
a whole gallery of sculptured heavens and hells
covered up to strengthen the monument.

Behind windows nailed boards
glass smashed and the boards signed
with love from Joe.

You are invited to squid on the worm gas
trapped within your own subjectivity
Vertical spears horizontally fixed
These harmonies of violence
an observer finds aligned to self-control
They let the cat out
to spray the illuminated
rattle traps
the lumber of an awkward estate.

Breaks

It is only themselves that they love intensely
We should think things had been turned upside-down
In 1981 he took the television aerial
Spun it around the room.
The Clown is ageless.

In the absence of a fixed masculinity
a jellyfish formed on the screen
Its position made ambiguous by movement.

The process of recovery gives the impression of absence
The self consists in my thought
I became that image in 1985 at 7000 feet
spinning in a light plane
Without weight
until continuous postural adjustments
and matches against surroundings

The definition of the other being a disease
nerves burnt the orientation
Unsure of gravity's alignment and
relationships to position.

From experiences of satisfaction
buried out of sight in the depths of their rest
the vertical and horizontal
were assessed by reading
an instrument panel under the screen
as the gauges notated lean.

Searched for the correct distance
outside the aircraft.
On his jacket
below the spine,
painted in gothic script,
the word 'Discharge'

The represented figures turned
Side by side, their likeness makes laughter
and rotating the painting allowed
facture of the somersaulted ceiling.

Distress and pain of bodily sensations
as the Clown started laughing.
Ghetto-blaster
Police siren
Helicopter
connected directly to your system of
drain control.
Learning to skate in the summer
at 8000 feet
scrubbing the roads and housing numb
from itching petrol and picking habits.
As we went to press the condition
was said to be stable and comfortable
        Tests are being carried out on the
            ultimate effects of the bullet
            which entered her left shoulder
                and grazed her spine
        What we do have is a new type
        of inquiry under the new authority.

Hypochondria of the erotic
the basis of all this wretchedness
catches camera
face rattle.
A rotographic line of the landing
traces the culture ramp
Rifting in a rage crater or limping
at 7000 feet up
the blood blizzards
spiked on charred fire.

The Clown both observes and participates
catches a blur of planets
in a moving sky plane
and blushes from agitation or
the smell of vegetation
peached in a lozenge.

The importance of the purpose
This arrogant force which checks and dominates
handed weightlessness as an apparition of presence

At precisely the point that should have been under investigation
a slick of yellow fog
Impossible to tell whether position
was established on the basis of how she feels
or how she fits
her surroundings

To indicate the disavowal of lack
to stop living inside himself
he puts a daze into the
dial glass.
The vertical intrusion into the horizontal
combined into the overall queasiness
and the smaller breaths
The tension thus is between
stratification and breakage
between the island of the tonal
and growth.
Next to the Hall of Machines I suggest
they put a Hall of Accidents
train derailments
pollution
collapsing buildings
That's what I say in
The Aesthetics of Disappearance
The main idea is the social
and political role of stopping.

There are biological considerations in its favour
against jellybean repeats
It's as if the animal became domestic,
raged its fill out of preach hysterias
This ignites the battle sop of apology
served in pain by a Blockhead
formed infill for paralysis
the lag of television.

The correct distance is the opposite of the feminine
a hardening of the heart
remelts the lava
north of the missile site

A charging of the ego
as the radar light starts flicking
and drop out over a basin
into successive perspectives
We have breakfast and dinner at once
in a chorus of red and yellow
fast breeding the inset annals
at pinches of cursary reduction
We hit turbulence
Any diversity fuses gasps
Subdivides fortunes into the cash nexus
an invidious flexing
two yards off touchdown.

2.

Asunder in a giddy state
prattle raps
with stray elimination
leech the fat out
and sever binds of ligaments to sell role
frees barmies of violins
through a gridded fence
trapped within bones of subjugation
raw in vital switched on the worn gag.

Whether above or below
gas rashed the bored sigh
grinds wind hailed balls

Ruddered up to tension the movement
a roguery of skeletoned cupboards
I rake out the trash after the impediment
asunder in bed
to mistake the factural squandering
feather-felted to the tremor off an under-trap
fools glossering with faulter canes
Harm clocked on a screw rag to their failing

Bending the bucket, the centre lost
alignment and the text became obsolete
without definition of taxation
or graphic meridians

Starts heating from the cash pan
the Clown steps out
by transport cistern attics and
averies of vocal rations in formal
wizz. Puerile densities form
where density is figured by a two-voiced
vertical question trans-born or on tally.

All over London
lungs detect billowing's
free short runs in the
flattened lock
the bony ocular
bellow in a frisking vet
A severity diseased
on aired dissent
from a department baloney.

Election birds in the net housed
without
Without need to lock into personality.

Boogie Woogie

1. She came down road in a sponge hat
    Dazed but walking, I remember
    looking back
    Jewel-hit eyes in a snow storm
    On a swing in a garden
    by the windmill
    On the Cleaner's face
    timed light   administration
    Felt only as she recoils
    Innocent?
    I draw back from a kind Stranger
    She crosses a pond then one-legs
    on a rock
    Lefthand commence to rub
    arthritis
    I *feel* my Hollowness repaint
    the seen.

    Talc reinflates distraught
    breath box. Hey!
    That swing's for kids!
    Long experience watches, chooses
    epicycloidal profiles
    She inspects a torn button
    The train out of the city
    literarily prolongs shape of the city
    waves of lichens on burnt-out wastage
    Willow herb analgesics and
    nettle curatives for wheezing lungs.

2. A child smothered in toys
    skids a ski slope
    from the city.
    I think
    I was in the wreckage
    I think one of the survivors
    got me out.
    I go to the swings when I'm angry
    A cold hollow spot, an aching
    I could not *give up*
    Used ice for a ramp
    they flew into the garden
    The oscillation of balance, contraction
    and sprung expansion not obviously
    in rhythm
    You simply take
    speed and flavour enhancers
    with you.
    She takes my breath

3. All I could see hurt my eyes
    Lowered egg into water
    turned the timer
    It was as if she
    was in pursuit
    without letting hold of the Stranger's hand
    her watch across
    pulse skin movement
    zig-zagged into winding
    tension and elimination
    of balance knocked banking
    One system presses jewels for pivots
    into spring-supported bushes to absorb shocks.
    Worked 8 to 5 fitting condensers
    into salaried circuits
    Routes from the city ARE the city
    Take in the smoke and
    stare out the lights, This
    wreckage moves

4. with extreme regularity
    run urgency
    self–winds
    dreams
    with external sounds, perhaps a watch
    or rust–hinged gate
    regarded by market as Off–track
    naïveté, radicative
    depths.
    I think I was in the city, or,
    heard two bells sound a
    recovery of debris and satellites
    Sometimes a vast stretch of
    quiet, like a lake,
    interrupted by insurance jump–jets.
    A tendency to pattern connectedness
    away from external appearance
    Broomed stock
    market floor
    recorded tobacco coffee and steel
    Rest
    as an intimation of a future
    tracks the radioactivity which resulted.
    Asleep on the swing night into morning
    watched that perpetual feeling
    Coleridge imaged
    an animant self–conscious pendulum
    continuing in its arc of motion by the for ever
    anticipation of it.

5. Scrub marks across geometric floor
    record details of industrial health
    In the lawyer's office
    the Cleaner looked to
    the Stranger's wrist glow
    Ideas on the culture dreamed of
    dispelled.
    Lit another dog-end, moved
    tide scum over white ground
    laid brush into suds
    turned them grey. It adumbrates
    the slow noise
    the swing's squeaks
    almost exactly interrupt.

Bop

1. To see it simply isn't easy
   She came down road in a sponge hat
   calls in a focus then another.
   I pull Brixton
   one by one
   I pull bricks down
   I am the Cleaner
   and my hat takes in the weather
   just as my brushes impact an interface
   between hands and
   the lawyer's office, stock
   exchange, the railway carriage.
   I look back at
   who I am feel
   the emptiness.
   The sponge is not infinite
   but its limits are immeasurable
   You can't see the atoms if someone's
   speaking, I mean if I'd zero angular momentum
   I'd be spherical.
   Lying on tea-room floor a
   ball of energy, feet
   up and blood
   filled head.
   Violence begins with each of us
   to end it.

2. Even when we are not in love
   he is grateful for being loved
   without spoilers to drop the drag
   left two-storey windowless concrete
   on external vehicular ramp.
   The surgeon conducts
   intimate searches down the barrel
   of a double bogey seven
   If we thought his stretched hand was to greet,
   we now see it serving to fend
   off male fantasy
   Of course we were also
   right the first time.
   His watch finished and smoothed on his elbow
   underestimated radioactive waste
   The hot components on his tongue
   pepper the back of
   his mouth until
   whole milk sours the
   heat out
   of anger.

   In such a basket of currencies
   three people beg outside
   Brixton tube
   call up Amnesia
   on the Read-out

3. There a scurry
   a flight of stairs
   then a landing
   A flock of dogs
   hit pavement
   from the terraces
   Jebb Avenue garden
   lament on radio

salt onto
ice, maybe
accumulator like
Two people
on the wall
breaking bricks
from underneath
themselves until
Bell sounds
closure.

4. My end is in succession
    houses fall
    are destroyed
    considerations
    at 50
    on the by-pass
    walk past out
    onto pond
    edge soft
    weeds underfoot create
    apprehension and delight
    No flamingoes simply hay
    rolled into bales out
    of white flowers tree tops
    against bright grey cloud
    superimposing onto clear sky
    moving over the window buried
    in my innocence's abyss
    Radium mines, Papuan heads
    some milk of childhood
    Rebuilding this community
    could be another century
    Soaked to the skin in mud
    coat lost crawling the first
    lot of wire then three rabbits
    in front of nose the traffic
    seems endless
    why am I doing this?

5. This morning like a daisy
    Fast aircraft loud bangs a kid whistling
    Stood in shower of yellow rocks
    loaves of rain
    Fourteen million watts ten times a second
    I watch you write this
    from a metal cabinet
    steep roofs bright light
    basket cases with hoses
    in all those greenhouses
    severity of sentence predicted on
    a revenge index

    a support building joined
    at the upper level with
    two positively vented air locks
    change clothes in the popping
    decontaminate
    link to main computer
    a meal of bells bulleted
    all both Morning & Night is now
    a dark cavern
    14 tons of glass gather
    fossil light.

Coda to Boogie Woogie and Bop for Albert Ayler

Laid on his back
ache
a sudden leaves fall
many still
green
record their mitogenetic radiation
describe them
perfume
we roll on
throw our arms around
trees autumn
but never know this.
When you're young
it don't seem to matter
if you tear your
playhouse down.

8. Two poems from CIVIC CRIME

Cakewalk

The image of a woman frottaged
by the Burglar
to the wall shifts
with his attention reads
a bicontinuous sponge
with surfactant interfaces.

His cleansing gaze as he sees it
rapidly fluctuates the curvature
of her shapes. They begin to leave
the wall and spatter
the footpath.
The Informer's report confirms

they are metallic balls of
crystalline liquids sandwiched
in saliva honeycombs and
dynamically disordered into droplets
disturb the gravel.
Oh what a wonderful world.

Tries to stop it and cannot.
The variety of their phase behaviour
encourages a focus deception
His long range spatial ordering
fantasises a language progression
from colloidal fluids to crystals.

Their viscosity reminds him of impact prints
left on an exit window by his fingers
stained with damaged plant cells
traced in the virus templated,
the Informer notes, as a leukaemia copy
in one of the collagen gene's first intron.

There can be no question of wipe-out.
The gravity-induced sedimentation
of the image in its suspensions had
stabilised the Burglar knew it
in the language of the City's
sintered adhesion.

Simultaneously he holds court
in The Prince of Wales
traps concentration
rather than solitude
A single organisation
of informers feeds
the evidence mode

in the dole queue
at one standing pours
three pints into his head
Such lethean measure
lures
the material electro-chemistry
of his abandon.

He chooses to ignore any digital alternatives
Speaks of life in terms of wealth:
his nerves scan the City as its temperatures
pass the red index limits lighting the Brixton horizon
His neuronal evolution capitalises on the spatial separation
of proteins in the synapses of his cellular processes.

Away from the perinuclear destruction
in his cell bodies
to the subterranean horizon,
his holdings are achieved by macromolecular stabilisation:
a vocabulary trench
almost voided of the means to dredge.

Intricate spreads of nerve cell processes
spatially
separate
and immunise his semiological remittance
from
the expression of his pragmatic turnover.

Innocence avoids complacent
isolation because he didn't know
the quest. Singularity
relieved of all responsibility
because he is a fool
run by terror, nothing
whatsoever taken seriously.

All day toxics
the narrative in its transparent
cruelty in an effort
not to become what I behold
but a stalwart attitude
to sustain a disciplined day
does not dissipate inner shudder.

Return
to a Faraday cage
dizzy from the static
metal escalator
on the down slope
defines
incompleteness.

He lives in fear of breakdown,
in sensitivity of capture.
His skid turns from the calm,
austere garden
back to the consequences of
the City's transcendence of its glow.

He cannot teach himself
to ignore the
screams and riot outside
but evades approaching darkness in both
the garden and the City move against him
Explosion

Feels like shatter,
you thought, Feels like
implosion of perfection
made of itself.
He watches himself
gaze at his abandon
birefringent on the footpath.

A plantal condition of Beauty
a transient flower
which he stoops to pluck
The difficult
capable of depth without
a weighty solution
against reflection.

Having what is essential without
having enough
limits his desire and thus the image:
a ceasing of hope couples to a ceasing of fear.
The two of them struggle
in front of the local nightsafe.

As he watches he participates in desire transformed in greed
oriented so that what he sees occurs in the direction he looks
at the moment it happens.
The distance of its occurrence from him
measures the same rest framed memory of the image
such that all other components vanish.

Necessity, weight, value condition
but do not constitute
the work
what do you do?
he is asked,
Why didn't you
sign on last week?

Sailing on a mirror
with birds in front of him
he scans for a
boop tone
to check his idealism and its concomitant
realistic aesthetic.

To balance out the arguments for leaving well alone
the Mathematician acts now to prevent inflationary overheating.
The breakdown problem
of established intellectual frameworks for answering questions
begins at the apple tree precisely at five o'clock in
the afternoon ransacked the edges of innovation.

A reverberant repression
tunes results from interactions
which cannot be separately attributed.
Precise connections between
similar colour responses activate
specific connections between orientation responses.

Look at it! produces
a stimulus constellation.
Gunfire, 11.00 p.m., 17th July
His nerves image
labile charts
which change with use.

The image of a finger tip
in the Informer's somatosensory cortex
expands after a period of intense stimulation
encroaching by up to one millimetre
into zones normally occupied by the rest
of the finger and part of the hand.

The slender phase partition
separates the successful making of a solvent for stains
from the deadly compound which explodes at a touch.
'Hitherto I have preferred to endure toxics on
my fingers rather than run the risk of being
forcibly expelled through the window.'

Neurons overlap receptive fields
are modulated by the angle of gaze
the strength of the responses to the image
at a particular location on the retina
varies according to the positions of
his eyes.

A topographical image is not required
to get the readout of spacetime.
The neurons in the Burglar's facility
learn the association between
eye and retinal positions.
His neuronal operations are probablistic.

This perception
results from continual cross-reference
amongst a variety
of stolen properties.
The activity in one is shaped
by that in others.

In the garden projections from two areas converge in a third.
They do not overlap but terminate in adjacent patches.
His single perception of her appearance explodes
from specific ensembles of neurons
located in several pockets each responding
to a particular feature of the stimulus field.

He stands imbecilic
to report what he sees.
The depth of his endurance
an index of his necessity.
His balm is a wonder whack more often than sunlight.
To be everywhere is to be negatively capable in loss.

The accident rapidity
took an age to occur and happened
quickly
proportions exactly
mixed into synthesis in the chamber
received pressure mass then noticed
it was not implosion-screened.

His language response a free mirror
stimulated by sensations of distance separation
from a second free mirror and produces a
permanent deformation in a gravitational
wave-burst with memory
in which the wave stores the signal forever.

A possibility the author turns
away thinks no one else has to approach
the discovered gasp of appearance
as if persuaded by anticipation of sex
he leans toward
its ephemeral image embossed on the wall.

The investigation, the movement
in the trap of unconcern
That Paradise became a prison (unreadable)
shines to some
marygold my hands scarred from burns
of its perfected collective
its hypergolic shock.

No warning
no preparation had made
resistance possible
it simply happened inside
a joy it happened
and broke pieces
into less than recognition.

As she focuses
the Photographer comes to something
which to her is Beauty
and stops there
instead of winding the lens
into acuity

This delay
requires memory of the image spacetime
and facility for discerning difference
These requirements maps in the premotor cortex
One deals with the plan and initiation of actions
the other with their guidance and execution.

If the Burglar could take
a light rest without insouciance
what he found
incompatible with the garden spacetime
Some wild bird
a sensation smelt
as it lifted from the flower bowl

decided about what is essential
and had excitement
what is enough pleasure jaded
towards holocaust. No more disasters
no catastrophes no more dissension
Only resignation
All accounted for.

Turned to face the bark and tears
limited desire to cure fear
unchains prisoner from escort
influx from correspondence
gazing from grasping
severs threads
of silken tackle.

I make a broken delivery of the business
as I become intelligent
take in slack on a
reward risk ratio:
not free
and not forever.

Processes continually modify
my feedback and lateral interactions.
An ecology that rabbits biologically
impoverished situations
where the cortex becomes a map of the world
each sensory modality charts several spacetimes in

different runabouts with about a dozen images
of the visual suspensions and half a dozen each of
the auditory inputs and how it feels.
It is functions that are mapped:
single areas contain multiple trace groups
bursting in different dimensions.

The Engineer's nonsense
dispenses with
misogynist fantasy.
He watches behind closed flesh
Doors of incredulous gaze
screen an unfolding
elliptic umbilic.

Spat at the wall
at loneliness
through fragments into
loss of description
dizzy from static, you cry,
What was that?
withdrawn from my own affairs in particular.

I switch on the cage
Cells selective for wavelength are among
those selective for orientation.
On the footpath the Bikeboy separately notes
size, shape, colour, position and direction of movement
with one glance.

Mottling leaves the garden wall
becomes marble after marble
breaks the working
glass an intensity of pressures
stronger than hail
and rolling on impact.

Their similarity of direction
marks out a field of gravity
beyond the garden wall
Exclusive doors conceal a haze indexed yellow
Marble-pillared,
leather-bound, pied-à-terre.

The City's policy
whiteballed to ensure the Informer
runs into the right kind of people
Always a light flashing somewhere
Everybody is very tired
Earning a fortune

Desire and greed are matched
in a 'she looks beautiful' eugenics
A chain of electro–chemical reactions
summarises into
the will to keep up standards

An order to establish
an options exchange encourages favour
forces a go out produces the
image futures
without sites that could lend
such aspirations considered cohesion.

Camel Walk

The Photographer's image of the Burglar
separates in her nostrils
begins to heave
as he loses his marbles
When you know the smoke above the town
you know where you are
When you love the culture of where you are
you love the world
Towards the end of our life here
decidability clarified.

The proof based on the idea that
all that was possible to construct
capable of simulating others
produced a halting problem
Whether there actually would be
a stop or an eternity.

The plan was once to define
sequence as a whole number
expressed rather
arranged
as increasing numerical order
Each program assigned its output data
a diagonal run of this table
changing and the new run becomes
an unlisted number
corresponds to the output
of no computer program whatsoever.

You compare the state of presence
with fragments of what might have been
a middle disposition
or is it virtuosity's arrogance
at odds with the known the fraudulent
a sublime smoothness

dipped into an expected prism
a measured vortex
trammed with a cold finger.

In this rhetoric disquisition
the grisaille creed
frames each memory rose
stiffened by an old gas pipe
or the sensibility shifts
to command an older typeface
pestilence   the many-coloured smile
your breath fills my body
leaves me without desire.

But not blame exactly. The process
of vitality entrammelled in code
believing the promise
of presence, the optimum
spin of immunological certainty
where the good is prescribed
oblivious to greed
you begin your weight check
a simplicity that cannot be demonstrated.

The mixture of vertiginal
with lateral consequence or what
was struggled to achieve now sold
You steal the day and sell the night
unsure which is which
No wonder or turn towards the marvellous
Only toxic hysteria
raves into homeorhesis
until oblivion confirms what you wanted.

The image of your desire
snookered or shadowed
by its own presentiment

Old as the industrial tip
trampled over on the way
home from another yard run
Beauty and Perfection interchange
Forgotten almost at the instant
of synapse before perception.

Vigour and concentration
tangled in muscle traction
crushed beneath cell clots
into the equivalent of barking dogs
randomised by alarms throughout
the walkway as the trees are removed
The Fireman burns them with
hot wires and cage saws
adding the furniture from a skip on top.

The horizon lights up or
at least glows and a
row of us stand and watch
one last time before
our lease runs out
There's not much point but
some record this and hold
on to the balcony rails
to earth their tempers.

The learned thieves gather at
the Windmill and eat chocolate molluscs
Their calling is given reverence
When you join them the sky
is nearly dark but you call it
morning. You exchange open framed
mutation with a view to improve
the conditions indexed by an
ability to tell the time without external source.

I watch my own image burning
and melting until the globs
of my presence dissipate down the
footpath towards the
firing chamber. The gulley
that empties every time I swallow
and fills with your stench
The City men meet you there
and switch baskets.

There now everything is sacred
except rest and the pound at
the door echoes or repeats
until the sound has no discernible
break. Vigour becomes the only virtue
power-leaded into every microwave
plant until saturation is sanctioned
Stamped onto each window hatch
with the photograph of a mammal.

At last anyway it's just about over.
You break me apart before
the first shocks are recognised
The pressure build has been too slow
to purchase. Almost without
notice I leave the garden
and stay there at once
There is nothing I can do about it
There is nothing *to* do.

Selected Resources

Resources for *Ideas on the Culture Dreamed Of*

Abramowicz, Marek Artur and Nobili, Lociano, 'Are there black holes in quasars?' *Nature*, 1982.

Adams, Thomas, M., *The Master Guide to Electronic Circuits*, 1980.

Art-Language, Vol. 1 nos 2 & 3, 1970; Vol. 2 no. 4, 1974; Vol. 4 nos 1, 3 & 4, 1977–80; 3 collections –
Art-Language, eds. Paul Maenz and Gerd de Vries, 1972 (essays 1966–72); *Art-Language 1975–78*, Paris, undated; and *Art-Language*, Van Abbemuseum Eindhoven, 1980. The *A–L Ways of Seeing* issue appears as Vol. 4 no. 3.

Berger, John, *Ways of Seeing*, see Peter Fuller, *Seeing Berger, A Revaluation*, 1980.

Braddick, Oliver, 'Spatial frequency analysis in vision', *Nature*, 1981.

Catalogue, The, *An Index of Possibilities: Energy & Power* by John Chesterman, Mike Marten, John May, Maggie Murphy-Ferris, Nadine Moggs Seton, Lee Torrey, Jon Trux, and Joy Watt, 1974.

DeBord, Guy, *The Society of the Spectacle*, two different translations, Detroit and London, both 1977.

Dodson, C. T. J. and Poston, T., *Tensor Geometry: The Geometric Viewpoint and its uses*, 1977 (1979).

Einstein, Albert, A Centenary Volume, ed. A. P. French, 1979, incl. work from Einstein.

Griffiths, Bill, *Zippy the Pinhead*, postcard 1982 (San Francisco) and *Zippy Stories* incl. interview, 1981.

Hawking, S. W., and Israel, W., eds., *General Relativity: An Einstein Centenary Survey*, 1979.

Heisenberg, Werner, *Physics and Philosophy*, 1959 (1971).

Hofmann, Hans, *Search for the Real, and other essays*, 1948 (1967).

Jones, Dyfrig, 'First remote sensing of the plasmapause by terrestrial myriametric radiation', *Nature*, 1981.

Julesz, Bela, 'Textons, the elements of texture perception and their interactions', *Nature*, 1981.

Lu, Yung-Chen, *Singularity theory and an introduction to Catastrophe Theory*, 1976, Springer Verlag.

MacDiarmid, Hugh, 'The Kind of Poetry I Want' and 'Third Hymn to Lenin, for Muriel Rukeyser' both in *Complete Poems Vol. 2*, 1978.

McNamara, L. F., and Wright, C. S., 'Disappearing solar filaments and geomagnetic activity', *Nature*, 1982.

Misner, Charles, Thorne, Kip, and Wheeler, John Archibald, *Gravitation*, 1973.

Mottram, Eric, 'Ezra Pound in his Time', paper delivered to the 7th Pound Conference, 1981.

Noordam, J. E. and Bruyn, A. G. de, 'High dynamic range mapping of strong radio sources, with application to 3C84', *Nature*, 1982.

Open University Course Team, *Biology: Form and Function*, 1981.

Paik, Nam June, Whitney Museum catalogue, 1982.

Penrose, R., in Hawking/Israel.

Planck, Max, in Mottram, 1981.

Plummer, W. T., *The Pin-hole Camera in Optics: Experiments and Demonstrations*, ed. Palmer, 1962.

Reich, Wilhelm, *The Cancer Biopathy*, 1973.

Reich, Wilhelm, *The Bio Experiments, on the origin of life*, 1938, translated by Jordan on *Revealer Cassettes*, 1979.

Reich, Wilhelm, *After Reich: Researches in Orgone Physics*, ed. David Mayor and Mike Weaver, Vol. III no. 2.

Richter, Paul, 'Modernism and After' (an analysis of Clement Greenberg's and Timothy Clark's positions), *Art Monthly*, 1982.

Rosner, Robert, 'Activity in Red–dwarf Stars', *Nature*, 1982.

Rosner, R., Zweibel, E., and Trimble, V., 'Plasma astrophysics at Santa Barbara', *Nature*, 1982.

Russell, C. T., Rijnbeek, R. P., Cowley, S. W. H., Southwood, D. J., 'Observations of reverse polarity flux transfer events at the Earth's dayside magnetopause', *Nature*, 1982.

Sandage, Allan R., *The Red Shift*, 1956.

Sandage, A. R., and Tammann, *Astrophysics Journal 194.559*, 1974.

Thom, René, *Structural Stability and Morphogenesis*, trans. Fowler, 1975.

Vygotsky, Lev Semenovich, *Thought and Language*, trans. Hanfmann and Vakar, 1962.

Wilson, Kenneth, discussed in 'Has the Ising lattice come of age?', *Nature*, 1982.

Winfree, Arthur T., *The Geometry of Biological Time*, *Biomathematics Vol. 8*, 1980.

Wittgenstein, Ludwig, *Notebooks 1914–1916*, trans. Anscombe, 1961. *Vide*, for instance, 'The sense of the proposition is what it images'.

Yau, K. W., McNaughton, P.A., Hodgkin, A. L., 'Effect of ions on light-sensitive current in retinal rods', *Nature*, 1981.

Zeeman, E. C., *Catastrophe Theory, Selected Papers 1972–77*, 1979.

ZG magazine, ed. Rosetta Brooks, No. 3, 1981.

ZIG ZAG magazine, ed. Kris Needs, November 1981.

Selected Resources for *Brixton Fractals*

Angry Brigade, The Bombing of the American Express Building, street newspaper stand announcement, London 1983.

Beshare, Joseph C., and Iuvone, Michael, 'Circadian clock in *Xenopus* eye controlling retinal serotonin N-acetyltransferase', Atlanta, 1983.

Beuys, Joseph, *'Some artists, for example Joseph Beuys' multiples, drawings, videotapes*, California 1973 (including conversations).

Blake, William, *The Notebooks of William Blake* (facsimile) ed. David V. Erdman, Oxford, 1973.

Brecht, Bertolt, 'American Poems 1941–47' and 'Last Poems 1953–56' in *Poems Part Three*, trans. Anderson, Bridgwater, Bowman, and Willett, London, 1976.

Conrad, Joseph, *The Shadow Line*, London, 1917.

Crick, Francis and Mitchison, Graeme, 'The Function of dream sleep', *Nature*, 1983.

Dickens, Charles, *Hard Times*.

Einstein, Albert, *op. cit.*

Flaubert, Gustave, *Bouvard and Pecuchet*, trans. Earp and Stonier, London, 1954.

Frescobaldi, Girolamo, Organ music, BBC Radio 3, 1983: 'sudden mood changes; unprepared dissonances; rhythmic restlessness; jerky motifs'.

Gorz, André, *Farewell to the Working Class*, trans. Sonenscher, London, 1982.

Grinstein, G., and Toner, John, 'abundant phase transitions', New York, 1983. See Moulton, etc.

Gris, Juan, paintings in *The Essential Cubists* show at the Tate Gallery, 1983.

Halliburton, David, *Poetic Thinking, An Approach to Heidegger*, Chicago, 1981 (incl. fragments trans. from *Erlauterungen zu Holderlins Dichtung*, Frankfurt, 1971).

Hammitzsch, Horst, *Zen in the Art of the Tea Ceremony*, trans. Lemesurier, London, 1979.

Hayman, Ronald, *F. R. Leavis, a biography*, London, 1976.

Hofmann, Hans, *op. cit.*

Jakobson, Roman, *Verbal Communications*, San Francisco, 1977 (incl. fragments from Glinka, Kirsanov, and Voznesensky).

Johnson Diane, reviews books on wildernesses, *New York Review of Books*, 1978.

Kristeva, Julia, *Desire in Language*, trans. Gora, Jardine and Roudiez, New York, 1980.

Ladzekpo, C. K., interviewed by Melody Sumner and Sheila Davies, *Ear/West*, 1982.

Leacock, Eleanor Burke, *Myths of Male Dominance*, London, 1981.

Leavis, F. R., *vide* Hayman.

Link, Winston O., exhibition at The Photographers' Gallery, London, 1983.

Lotringer, Sylvere, edits *German Issue, semiotext(e)*, New York, 1982: work from Lotringer, Paul Virilio, Heiner Muller, Jean Baudrillard, Helke Sander, Martin Heidegger, Joseph Beuys, Michel Foucault, etc.

MacDiarmid, Hugh, 'The Goal of All the Arts' in *Complete Poems Vol. 2*, London, 1978.

Mallarmé, Stephane, *vide* Kristeva.

Maritain, Jacques, *Creative Intuition in Art and Poetry*, London, 1953/54.

Martin, Kenneth, *Chance and Order*. Drawings by Martin, Waddington Gallery, London, 1973.

Mayakovsky, Vladimir, *How Are Verses Made?* trans. Hyde, London, 1970.

Meyers, Jeffrey, *The Enemy*, a biography of Wyndham Lewis, London, 1980.

Miller, Richard, 'Made in Togo', *Strange Faeces*, 1974.

Misner, Charles W., etc., *op. cit.*

Moulton, D. E., with Moudden, A. H., Wilson, A. H., and Axe, J. D., 'abundant phase transitions', *Physics Review Letters*, 1983.

Nicholson, Ben, exhibition at Kettle's Yard, Cambridge, 1983.

Nietzsche, Friedrich, *Thus Spake Zarathustra*, trans. Hollingdale, London, 1961.

Nutrition Education, National Advisory Committee on, commissioned by government and subsequently refused publication. Article in *Nature*, 1983, by member of committee.

Palmer, Samuel, *A Vision Recaptured: The Complete Etchings and The Paintings for Milton and Virgil* (facsimile), Trianon, 1978.

Protect and Survive, HMSO, 1982.

Reid, Constance, *Hilbert, A Biography*, of the mathematician David Hilbert, London, 1970.

Russell, Bertrand, *History of Western Philosophy*, chapters regarding Rousseau and Voltaire, London, 1946 (1957).

Sweeney, Pat, interviews makers of *Carry Greenham Home*, Beeban Kidron and Amanda Richardson, handout at Cinema Action, 1984.

Tankas in the Gulbenkian Museum, Durham.

Tipper, J. C., 'Rates of sedimentation and strategraphical completeness', *Nature*, 1983.

Waddington, C. H., edits *Towards A Theoretical Biology: Vol. 1 Prolegomena*, 1968; *Vol. 3 Drafts*, 1970; and *Vol. 4 Essays*, 1972, Edinburgh and Chicago. (Incl. work from Waddington, Lewis Wolpert, and Christopher Zeeman).

Williams, William Carlos, *Autobiography*, New York, 1951.

Zeeman, Christopher, *op. cit.*

Zeldovich, Ya. B., with Einasto, J., and Shandarin, S. F., 'Giant voids in the Universe', *Nature*, 1982.

Bill Griffiths

SELECTED
POEMS, 1969–89

Contents

Introduction

Bill Griffiths' poems are dazzling. More than any work in English since Gertrude Stein they insist on being recognised as surfaces and structures. Statements are made. Stories are told. Places and people are described. A bitter anarchism is expressed, also a Nietzschean yearning towards energy and joy. Yet statement, narration, description and expression are kept in check so that the poem is seen as itself, a poem, an artifact, an edifice with an importance over and above its subject matter. It is not the light and the landscape, the sense of motion of limbs or machine, the anger and the disappointments, the passions and hungers, which are magnificent. It is the poem itself which, in Griffiths' work, perpetually dazzles and astonishes in exactly the way the great stained-glass windows of European cathedrals dazzle and astonish before the eye has recognised whatever image is depicted.

People are reluctant to allow words to do this. The image of Christ may be presented in a thousand fragments of coloured glass because glass, light and architecture are materials in which structure is expected to take priority over content. But words in their day-to-day function are the vehicle of information. If this priority is made secondary to their glory then a cautious and insecure area of the mind panics in case efficiency is lost in euphoria. To allow such a panic to determine the nature of poetry is to set poetry on a level with road signs and government white papers. Griffiths' work refuses such a levelling with aggressive vigour. Instruction manuals deal with facts. Poetry deals with excitement and joy. It may certainly inform but its first purpose is to energise, to exalt the spirit and kindle the eye. Griffiths' work is a vivid demonstration of this priority.

How does he do it? He uses a variety of language: prison

talk ('its sick fucked-up fish (that gave emselves up) jumped on the hookz'); biker talk ('Hey, Blue! Tell? / What cars a'like racin' at you'); dialect ('sow'd as a tapioca most / 'at curds-up or cuts in the tabby sky'); literal translation ('no-yes grass's semi-audible sweet-howl'); ancient English ('Unlovely come I here some knight / That would with monsterdom fight'). The literal translation places English words in unusual syntactical positions which present the text as form a fraction of a second before the content registers. Similarly the colloquial passages use phonetic spelling, obscure nicknames, opaque references, to delay comprehension so that form makes its unimpeded impact ('the grand bagged billy's eyes / strained out from the glass-indoors / at quaint manner of its ledding /an' loud earth-up'). Throughout the text syntax is playfully and/or sometimes violently rearranged into an unfamiliar and unexpected order: ('Art being or being Our Art Art beginning And art and starting-white hedge (be) doing Trigger tiger wide-bayed snowy-up is Yolk-yellow (girl) see deep Fella').

In the forms thus composed sound appropriates a major role. Rhymes, rhythms, alliterations, vowels accelerate, explode or dissolve in relentless, marvellously controlled sequences. Space and punctuation are used as silences, delays, percussion, or are withdrawn to achieve speed and smooth flow. Parentheses are opened but not closed. Sentences are begun but merge into other sentences before a full stop is inserted. A manipulation of phrase edges is used with a similar effect to that of Dada poetry. There are also similarities to the way in which a saxophonist like John Coltrane will rephrase a melody relentlessly, again and again, to find all the possibilities of a given handful of notes.

The sense, when it does burst through, comes enhanced, each image or event spun, polished, illuminated and celebrated by its membership of such a majestic galaxy. What filters through the myriad colours, chips of rainbow, frozen dew of forms, is light, the sun itself, life, sensibility and glory – 'Locked in in the beauty, Locked into the beauty, Locked in in the beauty.'

Jeff Nuttall, 1989

After Stroke

his jacket, boots kept outside the holding cell
I exhale: my breath tastes
as cut and raw veg
ceiling and great flanged tree
roundabouted, grudge
and wedge
the cuss-crush, bits of
death by fire, death by pneumonia, brain-jolting
with major wings
floods, catching.
slow angry I move
like with the heart of a hedgehog –
shocked with drink
Pete starts off to smash
the cell open, forgets it –
volcanoes=volcano will push the trees aside,
tilt and melt, like lightbulbs, till too
superheaven admits no light but a lemon blaze.
but it never comes / chains together,
mine
the similes leap
nothing of it happens
it wldn't happen, I suppose – morning,
I try to get my legs to move
Alf wakes with his hand in his belt
Pauline doesn't stir yet – thinking:
it wld be better to burn the money
than be caught w/ it in yr pockets

the cold roll of the rivet
the judged spark of cold stony flesh
the solemn spinkle of bells toward a sun
vast dimensions
pinewoods & pure roadways choose on,
don't check you

Alf and Thor – *Winchester*

Like reading stone (porridge) its sick fucked-up fish (that gave
emselves up) jumped on the hookz (by themselves) bacon (that
jumped into the pan) wakey wakey get down this here dark
corridor which is dining room which is porridge   letters (good)
Up there Thor
When he would raise sun (hammer), no?

And the Lambs

Larry hath
Sheep teeth open
(Well it's a white morning)
Sheep that will eat by bone
Jaws are grand axes

Uz is allays bein sinful Uz is fed up wiv it clamit Satan

And lamb

April Poems

20TH APRIL

Rocking and lapping
about
wooden train
this crass guy
on both sides of a horse
shakes hands
and extends an orange cigarette
there are walled cities to look at
a massive disinterment

When I awoke
Tiger & Panther, Lion, Leopard
slunk off.
'Me, I don't have dreams.'

22ND APRIL

A tiny insect from the counterpane
stepped into my nose to keep warm

27TH APRIL

Spring Medicine:
2 lemons
2 oz Epsom Salts
1 oz Cream of Tartar
1 qrt boiling water
Spring boats, gargoyles
were dashing
darting into the mouth of the sun

28TH APRIL

No home
Sometimes it's light, sometimes black. Distance now,
Orange bondsmen move aside for train
out of shov'ling and hamm'ring.
A pissy ugliness transforms the vault.
Who shall we turn on then?

The Argosy

Jason –
gold then almond
shone his puppet dress
against the grove-pattern.
A lover
that was his part
in the quest-sail

Gems
if they had djinns in them
sending out light
a fist-diamond
watery as a pear
light-sliced pink

Out in the rime
the ribs of ice-jokes
gem in the tarmac.
I taste ferrous air.
They are frozen, they are solid
all the stinks of London.
Landless dragons
deal out ugly rumours, all the same.
Or savager.

Like a dragon-quilt
my grass-scape, cress, aylett, & beside the water, comfrey,
'why it's like a walk in paradise'
say 2 gipsies, for our benefit,
as they're off to hatch a plot on some boat.
Yes, snake-neighbours,
let me hang the winter-tree with yellow bottles
not spells (love-worked moorings), folk,
to make you perfect,
just bearable.

It is fifty-three. The land floods.
Then the great lady   left her estate of dead birds
sped south   to screen her cognizance
for the deity denies evil   won't be delivered to bad luck.
Who would choose mud   above chalcedonies?
Who would not eat   exquisitely, talk in angel-speech
pretend there is nothing,   no weather?

I look in the crazy mirror
   it is fluid and thoughtless
      some are tigers' claws, combats, clouds,
         paniers of oats, all ugly, blowing and blown.

great break/burst of oil
searing the hot cylinder / the cylinder ribs
black cape on the shoulder tips
   age-dust to forearms
      shadowing the jeans
welding and bike and owner
its heavy carbon
all but life-holding
grease-coat and oil-hymn

Comets & star-pops
curl from my cigarette;
it is possible they will all be souls.

The purpose: glory of the word
The purpose: human sense together
The purpose: futures
The purpose: all how we work
Also: dinner-plates, laughs & fashions,
The patterns! & their erotic force.

Poised
to take a peach,
tho the studs of it prove skull-stones.
Locks that won't turn.
Snapped flower-threads.
Wd not, wd not
walk up
empty stairs
stairs from the bed
and the sea-bed

The seeds of peace
stirred into the fertile furrow.

The mud-million
slowly and slowly mo' imperfe't
re-forming
re-growing (unshowing)
slowing

A taint carpet
A music-wheel racheting over the shop
(sez) Will you buy me?

At the walk of the beast
the padding knife-plants turn, wait, acknowledge
and the woh-spined fox family, sods though,
sneer and slow and superior,
how the taddy-lights
marvel the spire-stand-grass.
It is shrieking, its pass
– who guesses what the hunter has ahead?

Aristeas' Journal

In the seventh century BC a Greek traveller called Aristeas seems to have made a journey into Scythian territory, roughly where Romania is situated today. He finally reached the edge of the Carpathian mountains, where he hoped to find a race called the Hyperboreans, whom, it was rumoured, were specially blessed by Apollo and lived in a golden age of peace and contentment.

Evan Hadingham

Like as in Greek democracy
I wasn't voted or elected
but picked by a chance,
lotted to seek out knowledge: starts and meanings

I found many fragments

Sea-veined
sky-gloved
star-haired
every heir
and all
settling
to be the world.

He says he lays him, acts horizon, has the quick earth
    power to back,
She says an arch, she will arch her' like a packet-sky,
    to be earth-over.
And he rises
She opens
A rehearsal of how to make
Make / to Do.
Warm world living about
Between the two, still.

Two codes
two keys
Certainty
Stability
The all million–long continuity
(like races of ferns)
Handling complexity
Admitting variety / unpredictability
(all the potential & quasi-new pattern of an unrolling carpet . . .)

One moment there is wheat, then a wave.
In a rush you trust some people
But they are a cold window to.
You had better save your
loyalty sez the sandstone figure.
But what then?

Then we are as of but a
cold wall
            ahead us,
where we 'ttack & break at
with dumb knobs
like we could burst beyond,
see the halls and homes others share in.

Or
bead and rod
everything to a trust
a joy
and a world–crush.

OR
what holds us?
(faintly painted
pictured together in a time)
Nothing?
(walking to the next adventure, room to room)
(Just lots of tunes to listen to)
(A dangerous floor)
(It is a good game)
(It is a bitter drink Eve served.)
(It is not like being a football fan.)
(It is like being tuned in to the rain.)

These are the wrestlers of agony
dislocating their ankles,
tearing, in a pair, in terror, yelling,
squeezing, sick in the struggle
to annihilate,
pull open the puzzle, WHAT IS IT? WOLF
or with a shake of sweat from the eyes OR LYNX OR
laugh to be left laying SOMETHING? FORCE THE
   PELT AWAY
twisted under the victor, panting derisions, FORCES
try rise, heaving into black. BLOOD FROM THE VEINS

Body-verbs
that are muscle, that are moving,
to lever shaft to shaft; to guard, to grow,
Blood-fed the bulge of the arm pulls up
/ anchors
or the leg folds & straights to run.

A leg-ring
a wrist-bone
a chain
as tho' you can box-up action
unwire the arteries
& still be classed sensate

Lacking sexuality to violence;
more when its risk arose
between units that could or would not breed
a speci-al or political obliteration.

Why the world! – a regime of calamity
            (At your imagined –
Where each subject thing risks its neck
            (coming to impossibility

(Today
      Lit by the little bunkers of gas,
      I wait,
(The competing is
      the whole room square senses,
      what is settling, coiled,
      the great, quartz-scaled snake-being
      of the cold
      tight & bright
      so when I bed, mid-black,
      that will be soccy,
      boox, flowers and I,
      in the race to reptile,
      the stately unheated hole.
(Today
The competing
's over.

And by the fields
red & raisiny, a blur
that are people to run

Against the sky-etch / snow-arch
snow-land at football,

the	RUNS	footballer
all turn	SKIDS	like a herd
roused	SHOOTS	in tremble
alert	YELLS	ice-active

ice-show-er
surges forward / scents it, the
22-footed dragon coils itself to goal
will (to) trick the goal-girl
in her adverts (it is of a, the, same)
loudness of body-drama
& the spring of the action
the snowy steaming crowd.

The Hittites invented letters
but it was the skalds linked words
like gold–rose–wrists of new–shirt–smartness,
Or goddess–tears (for rain) and share–singer

The lovers
like wrapping a parcel

   caring and folding
   these are the leaves of lettuce

   a smattering of diamond light
   still in a box, perhaps

   but a glowing pepper–burn
   rubs teeth & boot, breath, belly

   accepts, receives,
   folds, saves, rolls rose–in–like (lives)

A crisp route,
mountains,
parallels of rock, shine-faced,
austere & sun.
A pass. I pass. Loose-slide.
I will make it.
Interviews with Hyberboreans
in their cloud-rooms, coming.

The dust's shipped
on the earth-shoulder;
the barbarian
is grass now
& the knees 'come bricks.
The mists ring us,
are vertebrae, star-bones,
a sensational rising.

That we dissolved, awake,
was show-token
would you think you one –
more a collar of tawny orbs,
star-board
that incessant bless,
patrol to one, will-less &
king-loud

flesh-loquent
the air-buds arrange
new compounds, old word & new word
a juggling cups, beans
tumbling, shipping to the dust
mazed as mute as complete

Barcarolle

I am watching
sitting graves (and)
between sky and sea
rich blue of rocks,
between boats
the lord that looks along
all the levels of the oceans
eats the workforce
happy as rails,
there is smoky glass goggles to see
on the dark green and flowing sea
and in a orange-shaped round boat
confusion of lungs as
lime-like oak-leaves
within, abeach
a thousand sands
colour in, the tubes are a
monster chewing itself
a sheet of planes
made of nuts and nails
tells you
cheer up in the winding ear
be ennobled this dead work
also
there is a vast chain is the coast.

for Bill Compton

Viso, ha'in' seen Dover, gaol of sorts,
To spewing
And sixteen – shit
Non-warring or running – nothing,
Folk cutting my hair and japing me,
The cliff and the kids thought me
As I'ld –

At Bill's house (looking the finch's eggs) as that who took his
studs first (sling 'em keep talking – know – was you hit than
going in – bang – you gotta keep them off and you gotta make
mates good but the laugh the Pakis just being fisted in the
corners shouting stop and stop

                        that's Ashford

Cold and come out the clothing from the box stinked yep

        Indulge no'is pater
        YES PATER
        And I get real hurt and unguarded
        Cold (it was bad) (I put it)
        Lost, little lamb!
        Looking for stones
        That is weighty and then sharp yeah
        Or money
        Or job, pal

In the market-bit waiting for you to join in
A' left scared SILLY.
    All the cold of Christmas's gathering
I get to think
My jacket being dry up of blood, pretty proudly and –
DOMINE
Gotta watch Saturn at eating, and everything, says he
   won't stop
Panting and gaping: littly
And laughing in circles, yard o'
Bone-eating, screaming,
Man, do sum'ing

But me – colours writ open my back
Worked the fair – foke dirty-faced
And Sarratt – November – ice jawed (said give us
   a hand Billy!)
That and this moist weather, egg-sweating, stalling,
Firing half-so, tatty, tamed, where's she
Bathing off my ears

Di – es! Time torks your hair – do I know? – for the worry
Thru the gaol-jaws YOU SEE the mess of everything,
   ain't anything but a mess.

Birds (*found text)*

not fast
70 m.p.h. may be about their maximum
                                                    an
imagination in setting

ready enough
to call yourself a liar
to make a special study
                              or
their love of singing in wild weather
singing on the roof of Iona

in many cities
ripening grain
corn, engines, many another

there
by means of coloured rings
food-sources
Kale and root crops
                              maybe
adapted
helped to hang on
disappeared

these lists give us
total counts
week-ends, half-holidays
chief cause
                    How / when
by means of
for me
two bits of ivory
one with a toothed edge

living
criss-crossing
is more of
tolerably regular
archaic
anywhere near you
seen at sea
                informed
Archaeopteryx
towards the end of the 19th century

means missing
worth making
                iris
the human shape

brecks newest
recent
number
rare and flourishing
'unspecialized' 'equal' 'good'
                                        was
in the war
a high-pitched 'chizzick'
summits of
gears or gorse

visit
vor wanne snow lith thicke and wide
an alle wihtes are close and spiteful
                                attend, such
more hints
of rebuilding

there is still the chance
for
any young Londoner
to
make a name
by
a career of conquest
unequalled by any other
make good
good subjects

The Boat

The tomato and the orange check my shirt
My boots are made upon the beach
Past all the castles of the south or north
The 'Cimmerian' is the finest craft

The cars roar as leopards in a fight
My folk are dead, my son-kin live
The fierce heatless sun fires the roofs
In the dark we start off for work

She will not lack for sense or skill
We will use the sky for fuel
Her hull is made of doubled steel
And Crom will guide her keel

The Bowmen

We stand
naked shoulder
to shoulder
by the cattle-pens.
The clouds
move sometimes
away from
the Sun.
Sometimes its flaps
play bright-white
or sombre
on the peacocks
that belong
to Mazda's brother.
I (it is my job)
hold
the loop &
torquer.
someone else
is expert
who has warmed
the coffee gently
into
the cups
and then loox
at the time on his arm.
At the water pump
and its dark site
the
close Archer
makes right
& I go loose the
bands or belt.
Like an arc of beads
the red birds

spray up
in target
so safe
the whole field
enters
is entered
it is a sharp sort
of rite this,
not for playing or
moving,
look up
or laugh
before return
I mean, to concentrate
till the
dart is off
& I press
away lest
they land soon
I don't even answer
in the rush
of wings
being too busy
as he knows
sees
as Ahriman
sways in the air
in a pure room
of outside
then he's his own
T-shirt off
and beating upward
by when
I can work for him or not
as he needs,
or draw a coil maybe
when the main flock

break
& spar a bit at their low feet
for which is harder
till the very last
or latest
is made free
is away
with the wishes of a joke
sometimes we're
wood-sawing then
or anything good

At Boxing

Art being or being Our Art Art beginning And art and starting-
white hedge (be) doing Trigger tiger wide-bayed snowy-up is
Yolk-yellow (girl) see deep Fella

> Shorts / navel
> Shoulder complex arm complete
> Olive-fist (ban'aging) go grand-red gluv
> With ribs crossing canna whale
> Sox boots
> Getting help

bang BELL tanned tabor Sure-ringing gulling Gross game
Chesting And roped real hoarse mouth move see Old smell
New-smell Poisoned shirt Pausing Baby box Thunder-wagon
thanking god Rub girls feet Shouting-touting Large grey
Ring-side-size me outside is-me here is you
REX or
oooooooooooooooooooo
oooooooooooooooooooox

> Sitting at gurl
> My private nose to;
> Long flutes of (tlips) tulips, silly, says?
> Az no ideas in power
> Sometime stop

Was training to train sweating by heart square-hearted tramp
and toot an' ache excizing lax day tanking thinking eye-aim
suss marigold thirst-wrecking wham orange gut-trucking brain
gains spit it my heart is olive-shape and stone-shine a boars and
wolf-cars to: pink chalk tap-skip tumping bag red-balled run-
good and over and foun-tain blurbs or pain be'n but plastic
    Tomorrow when
    Dead is validated I talked to dead Dead licked my skull too
(with

> no
> indignity)

    Graded, as
Starting on the great sand-firing-spiral.

Brunnhilde & Me

cartoon beauty
the children's world of Wagner
sequin-chatter / double-glassed
and the ardour of quest
mazed between green frost-trees
book-cliffs
sun-coloured clouds.
Our arms with the softness of bread
hold & hold

hooper-squawk
grit-tufts
crystal-twinning wings
sand-mat and bristly
a bird
          to announce
the secrets of language
think-gloat and deep-glass
charm-conversant,
                                     whole

Echo
with both hands
trap-carrots the conscious-ty.
a circle of time
re-rehearsed and re-re-rehearsed
in continuity
a rhyme-road
super-emotioned, drunken, heroic

A path between square-lights
sloping, beamed,
sun-wood once and coal-headed
a twisted child-show of Pinner,
once light-skewed, again
a shade-shop
and the planes broad and hot
art-stopped
then crooked in a fairy-wail.

Building: The New London Hospital

FRAGMENT 1

Adventure
big buildings / mountains
cartoons

Alf who was always sleeping in strange places

50 KG more than $\frac{1}{2}$ a hundredweight
my back adds it up / spinal sum

a bishop can hold an abbey in one hand

trial chord
a boot shot out the door with a yell
there was a 2nd boot
& a birdcage

ya he screamed
drumming on the chute and too
rushed round to grin on the levellers
maybe they like it, that humour

A VISION of
Polly Polly notion
for own wife, came into

FRAGMENT 2

                sometimes
I think it
you don't understand me anymore than I do you

all over the city
the contempt is statue
– statute
like the frixion makes unending is

4 or 5 trumpets in a Shaker hymn
and McNee is on telly

the honour
oughtn't to hide

I was awake a worker
as of bricks w/out straw, gotto

the great slabs or sills mad as hell
I rolled em uphill rather than lift em
still they caught me so I was eating blood some more

it was strength I
wanted to show, not
blood

FRAGMENT 3

In cold (temperate
to / is open to
sunlight.
Be sure that
air, esp.
Suit
and farmland
can
or
which is cheerful, firm and dry

FRAGMENT 4

little Jo wakes me up
with kick a little poke a kid laugh
I go an' twist Alf's feet (a bit more malice)
later bang on Pete's window
an come an try an think up an excuse for me.
No.

Each order's a
puzzle.
maybe I work my own work out.

Scrape on out

beeches
whizzing by
reddish red
my new boots
are as good as gold

SHEPHERD'S CALENDAR

I follow her into the front room
I leave the sheep in the back room

what wld be really good
go an' sell all Tong church

wolf in one hand dog in one hand
no it's useless to separate 'em

everyone wantz a party
today I pretend I'm counting

to be helpful
I lead all the fish up-river right into the boats

maybe I shld get back even
to shovelling the sand

hang on
try yr head in the helmet

FRAGMENT 5

SILICON
legend of glass mountain

Three kinds of sand are commonly dug: red, white
and black. The red is best, white is adequate,
black not so good.
If there are no sand pits nearby, you may get
sand from riverbeds, or the seaside – but sea-
gravel is difficult to dry.

Some buildings truthfully are silly
Abbott's Hotel
a kid and a big thick fork
shiny and soapy and frothy
plaster all over like the sea'd been in
across the road

'this beach this is
hot heavy tortoise
into a
LYRE
a letter, a windmill-postmark'

'Here
the buildings broke upward like chained paper
piers & pattern-glass but grey
steady half: Imhotep.'

FRAGMENT 6

more of I equals less of I
more of mine equals less of I

Alf says you alluz wake up before you die
since all dead people have open eyes
or iz it muscle-relax
or ties into
nothing but life

FRAGMENT 7

a easy rattle sound
the morning
the flights, spirals
sweat gently in the chill
as easily ride horse on
up the glass mountain
pawing in the sand
sand as wall, as window
like a set of sums
fits up

why not goodwill? you survive
if it's fuller of people than bits – no harm
even in the middle of a swimming-pool
I still know my own feet.

The soft-bread man
the sandman
the fireman
all working all day around

how do we know we shall ever dye, I said and began to
    laugh?

observe / play the blood out my finger
like a conversation

O ———, may you live forever

FRAGMENT 8

atop
set of seeded   in the morning
a settlement   when the wood of
a family of children-bldings   the stairs was
lie or wait, children seem to   new & washed
                                       to rails

chal
kravine
what a great scene – crevice
flick here, there
the stunt viaduct enz
a loop iz the stomach
shit you, I smoke
c'lyx-studded, a roll a roll a roll

watch out
what passed
it was
now the four ties are in place like a gong
wait

more I run
what an air
this a laugh
public an'
survive

FRAGMENT 9

1 go to Zoo
   draw
   watch Telly
   play
   hope me Mum wakes up
   read me a story

2 coat
   two
   three
   two
   coat
   sweets

3 go to sleep
   settle stomach
   go to market
   buy boots
   visit T'ronto
   go to seaside

4 go out tonight
   go out tomorrow
   go out for a ride on a bike
   get a new motor-guzzi
   move

FRAGMENT 10

what a lot of make, take, break
why did you take the job?
jump over me then
fuck it I'll find out tomorrow &
think a bit of the pay

dwellings, Lord!

Try crow-scarers, right top a scaffolding pipe down
all the way, well or fantasy

FRAGMENT 11

My latest thought brick for an abundant supply for home and
clothes is being magnificently met. We have all had lots of new
clothes and many items for our home.

I find it amazing how many of my thought bricks are fulfilled.

My latest thought brick has just materialized. My young son
has been made a member of the local golf club.

I have had so many thoughtbricks . . . I was asked the other
day if I would take over selling a special piece of equipment.

Even my thoughtbrick for a new sewing machine . . . one is
now on its way from a friend who no longer needs hers.

A skin complaint has cleared up . . . in response to thoughtbrick
techniques.

FRAGMENT 12

For example, taking the cement onto palettes, for the hoist

For example, c'lecting the droppings to the chute

For example, catching bricks to stack

For example, carrying the long trunkings down the steps

For example, eating bacon

Shifting the poles under the skips

Smell of dust, cloud and chaser

Watching chasers moving about masks

Piping, shaped to wiring

C'lecting aly too, some little copper

Just LIFTING some things

FRAGMENT 13

Maple
oak or ash
chaff or sawdust
lime and two of rubble

mask of rust
red vest
(catch the brix)
not o'molten blood

FRAGMENT 14

discard of jacket / socks
yellow shirt & teashirt, jeans
Aren't you coming to bed
Hey come on to bed now
she oughta
or habit, like embarking
self super water
for to swim
series, series of wheats / fields
series of points, pennies
like, bulge
. . . .
shout sometimes
. . . .
pages and pages of writing

sweat starting about the ears
pumping 'bout lifting
in compression of the stomach (get or hoist)
near like cracking of the skin, on massive move
near hold of balls, placed, clear of drive of back
other shapes quick thought of, hello
strict neck in the swing of all the shovelling
that slews on around
tight to seams
it all soaring of the soles of the feet

sez 'as I ran the corner, face up straight this other guy one
more of them, guessed he was, took the bottle & broke it,
hard as shovel, again on him or choking up his throat, like
a struggle with nothing, swabbing the stones by, grabbed that
great block-lance-iron 'case of, but it was futting nothing more
there, swung the iron onto top so to lay it, what a distance'

FRAGMENT 15

great black grim were torches
with the lateness

unspeaking
like a flicker

a murmur of
bronze
the power of
the dim stars, grim
their black bulks

naked
wedge-shaped
thick neck
wrenched
whizzed

black-arched
curious
black stone ledges without a railing
lofty all sides

1st frame: the door in a sheer curtain cliff, amphibially flat, and, you can see, the door stands open.

frame two: a round hall, walls glow, a lofty-roofed, scare-image-laden building, & he follows them & around

frame three: a cavern of huge tiers, larger and more slow than any before, the walls studded, where / there squats, lo! reincarnated

frame four: a ledge, a fantastic scene, a natural bridge, in an instant, some interior gulf, frame behind is lost in

five, six, seven from bottom theatre to blue-roof-cabin, blue
tunnel out to a big bulb of daylight . . .

CUT THAT OUT, YOU! THAT'S ENOUGH! SLOW IT! SLOW!
SLOWER! DON'T LOOK SO SURPRISED! GREAT DAY IN THE
MORNING! I CAN TALK AS WELL AS YOU! BUZZ OFF YOU
GRUNTS! I'M SMART ENOUGH TO GET MY OWN FOOD IF I
WANT TO! YOU! WHAT'S THAT YOU'VE DONE! NO, YOU FOOL!
NO! LOOK! THE GORILLAS ARE BRINGING UP –

FRAGMENT 16

Useful metals there include twin sheets aly / lead.
Then the guy wldn't take his tea, after saying about spiking, it
wasn't, he's smiling, like . . . Other says, hey stop c'rupting my
brickies.
Could be bright.
Most, tramping about azin dunlop steel-plated boots, the real
trouble, now, boring, I thought fuck I'm fed up with it so I
altered my watch.

FRAGMENT 17

The fog
shut stop
all the work, some of it,
pick up brick-ties
. . . .
Notion . .
got it wrong

must be time to sleep

yep
time
evade
what a tyranny of fixed sleep, eh?

outside
learn to point
mix, six to two
not wonderfully right this
think of your own wall tho'
well,
tricky

full as the sea is clean

gild a new pit-blue tie-pin

FRAGMENT 18

Met Noel at Cheshire Street
out of boots my size

freed somehow of my jacket
out of my boots
now I can see you, it's sunshiny

SHEPHERD'S CALENDAR contd.

A rich jigsaw'd gorse
ruby / lamb-yellow on a sandy land, & dry lunch

surrounded by a 100 wheeling dinosaurs, at
an aviary

gaunt legs of rubbish, pliant of bone
set up working under the rainarch

looking to see what is out there

Changing Over

The decaying grasslands of rocky Koth are green
even in the glow of the fast-constructing dawn.
Soon my eyes pick out the types of white and the grades of
    other colours
it is a stunning matchment, esp. the grades of red or rust
beyond the normal stone / iron – forget the garden.
The travelling TV's-down and stopz like
a little layer of dust perches on the bone boat.
shells like wood shelter
paths and plants
radiating round for a child
leaving you lolly-lung'd like a cherry
that, all Barham Park
like Canons, not a thing there still:
big walls and glass-outed holes
all one new united space. Shelah.
It is hopeless to even query
where the bricks have gotten to.
a process . . .
In no. 02923, Elric the guest hero reduces Yagala
to a spangling ruin.
Outside where I'm travelling, the rain is reducing to snow,
and the snow to sunshine, like big blocks.

Chant

Lo the loud the
let the
over the dead, riding . . .
loud they were, yes, loud,
Screya! loud in the rooms
such sound
sound mine.
One-minded, them,
sole-thoughted liars
who rode me thru my land.
So shield me you
Screya!
Shields you are
Christ!
yes, sound-stoppers sound-starters
what me?
Out, go,
out
spear-shout
shooter, calm, settle it,
land,
if you're in here
what, look the,
loud,
look,
dead-hill, out
beat
off
what loud they were.
I stood under a shield
light
bright, how!
that,
set-haired liars,
half-headers,

when the strong strangers
told over what was doing
(reach throw wade row)
done
are you shields then?
the mighty wife
making
street-sound,
tell over,
liar liar liar
what you do, you.
here
head, look, head,
Screya!
Yelling, yelling
let the, make the,
spear-speed
and they
shouting they sent
where
where sound
I
them
other one
back again
gotto, will
sound/send
loud
speeding spear
screya!
or face
or front
throat
stair
wall
stock
parapet

long live the
let
stand under linden
lope along
hoo–riders help
very light ones
loud they were
out
spear-part
if
they are
you are here still
again now
spear-ones. scram.
sat the smith
struck
struck out
sword or sax
sound-maker!
screya!
little loud rooms
what! wounds those?
iron them?
head hold
have my shield
whole hall
hæftling loud
louder be
la
look
screamers
screws
screya!
what for
what wounds
what
iron

loud the
out
shout
spear if you're in
six smiths sitting
planning on
thing
they made
spears for slaying
work that
out spear!
not in not in
no
in sound in
it if
not any iron
steel-surround
work of witch
whole yellow
you
melt-you
must melt
it if was
hide-graze or heart-kick
vein-way
life-spinner
life-spiller
screya!
so you never
so there never be
shout
sound
shout
sound
sound-shouting
lo look loud lo.
against with

lords or laws
against the witch-one
this *shield*
for *sound*. Yo!
Can you climb
at all?
Ban then to
mountain-tip,
stay whole,
hale be
and who hears you.
Soft-speakers
down
are
as yo-yos.
Or faced,
fought,
as no slow stomach,
none shallow shoulder,
land-shouter.   /
                                  / yo! /
                                     /

Climaxes

What I want to set is language – STET

Only working in the dark iz a – WOLF-POET

The cycling old melody goes country-like – ROUND & UP

Where is their logic? Why they are no more than – HIATUS

Professionals? Ah – the little LICE-PODS!

Misery and woe to spiders all over the WORLD!

Just let a little sun come up, big enough to show me FRIENDS

After someone's death, stumbling suddenly into an open PLAIN.

White in the ice-light but also showing their red BOAT-BOOTS

Hunting thru the cow-fields for the quietly-confident MUSHROOMS

Panic screams thru his horns, collapses the LUNGS

The frost-ghost has left nothing but his claw-marks on the WINDOW

So strong the air was by these sharp rows and hedges, as ROMAN

Opened, it sinks, a heavy load of melted SOLDIERS

Water and wood and fire are bodies, but TOO FAST

In the Coal-Year

In the hot, the long
summer
the air was marked
with a bilious, flat smell.

Some rammed their
arms
into the cannon
to stop them.

Or said
'they will only fire
water'.

A 1000 goats-without-horns
ran up to the gate
waving their arms against the lorries.

They dodge to the right, the left, the right
Some are knocked flat

Some make a 'ground-kiss'
Or turn & turn like tops

It is an announcement of drums:
'aux champs! aux champs!'

Even the telephones
are a code.

Work is blockaded from the mines,
coal is blockaded from the steelworx,
the coal-trains are halted as they go,
the lorries are fired in the haulage yards,
they sit in the pits, block the bridges & towns with cars
and the centres of the dominion are ringed round,
occupied

The great flags
show the helmet & the horseman,
a red sky,
backed with spangles,
flutt'ring & winding sure
For Sogbo is the protector of flags

In the dark place
between
work-end, work-start, food-work,
in the time of drums,
polyrhythmic (for souls)
A THOUSAND YEARS OF COAL

'Aizan! Aizan, hey!
The stupid man ties his horse up
The intelligent sez he will let him go.'

Wash in hot water –
like tents of white &
full of flowers

begging,
a body rubbed with food,
small coins are kept under the ears,
and the necklace is put away
and their possessions
are free from the brutal & chaotic.

How can you come past
the birds on the poles?
the eggs in zigzags?

the eyes are plastered with blue
the boot beats on the tar
the crab & the snake & the helmet

Three-horned-Bosu
with a thin child jutting from his skull,
he
was carried with them into slavery.

To a land
that too shook,
shook, and
the hills steamed, smoked
(it was their own war-time)

Shouting then
(like scoring)
they make march
to the sea-board
skim their corn & flowerpots into the blue
To null the great force of the Ocean:
what will She do next?

In Colchester

A soldier steps along,
incredibly oblivious ov an anti-soldier
dogging him, shop-door to door.
Beer keeps the soljer-molecules together.
Anti-soljers make a pile of slates on the roof as they work.
Sometimes there is a collision.

Cugel's Tribute

When woke
athirst FOUR fiery gas's as
hair-ruby
magnet-knee

broach of roof
is: shoulder-free.
certain.
wires, choirs, pyres, fliers
are are
mo' magnified thru and by.

the blast:
winds, winds' caves, sacks
sagg'd,
cool, are's, lung. child
'at is in
these shreds across
– like a labour – sky.

No longer possessed, Glory –
sure, shoal, speak-unlike,
steer or all-bake, t'ward beak-ball.

A sunny blank.

all
allabout
tearstained rows of iron

clinch
and change (with you)

Cure

I am white as flour-paste (skin, limbs)
Then aglow amber, seaweed scented as I heal.
Sickanwhole, sickanwhole I build me like a coral
. . . chest . . . flat flesh

tall, pale
leafy a eucalyptus place
top perch
upon mazy or misty river-way

tussles of rope
cow-pats
smiling parties pass seaward

So I am seeking
gentlish herbs
to right
my sinning self

Kaolin and oranges

feelinglessness . . .
into the blue go
buildings and fog
what do I/you care about . . .
there are baked-egg and sandy-coloured banks
nerve and lip, toe and nipple
all clothing over emotions of a Hindu mountain, black by
    vegetation

body shocks
jolts of blue and

out of the rain
pretty young parrots sing and play

Cycle 1

(*On Dover Borstal*)

Ictus!
as I ain't like ever to be still but
kaleidoscope,
lock and knock my sleeping

Within
the complex of the fort against the French, Dover,
's mighty imperfection: fits to the sea,
the moat (and ported, kinging the blue, closed, so built-made
    and the salty grass and rubble of chalk growing
writing the chalk – kid
shout for separation

The ships, turquoise,
cutting open the sea
smiling killing
OK

The day opens up, is pale;
opens free, to me
my hands lightened, head

At running in the sun
I thought
this serious, my world is.

The sky blue
the barbwire is German
it is made with razorblades.
buckets a strong yellow

Do you know it's the sea?
the speaking sound
and I woke like a dragon's dream
taut-limb around and my teeth were avid
in wonder

The gross gates got to
fit
like clothing fits

You're you
and I ain't anyone but you

The bright crazy rings in agate
spring is.

The flower was forced open by the sun
is yellow of bad brass
like I beat it golden-black

Rowed up in roads, housing cuddling, cold
sky's lead's closed low of fear
just keeping crying
gets punished: punched by the sea
shit on by the rain.

Got trumpet you
screaming as an elephant
dog, fist, ground
god of an hiding

The days excrete themselves in summer, one, one, one

My feet are convicted are
prisoners in prison boots

En regardant vers le païs de France
on lanes of chalk
drumming
losing all the words, the shapes and
circles part

I think on the pattern of an action
till the gold of the answer I can beat anyway

Kid stood stretched like a unicorn like poster
as who anywhy wants?

The frost in triangles about the fort
is large as the fool sun
powerful
as sun.

Cycle 2

(*Dover Borstal*)

Morning s'blue
early, edgy, special
lay like a gun
in await
some sort sun's exploding

now
holy spirit!
unmother, diseasting
gotten to rolling, bowling
live, wide, wind
loops aerial bear

slipping all out
my dog-brain,
cancer-snouted to
the zagg'd teeth of the sky.

as a beaut nose-shouting horse, swervy,
outrunner
by blue
my head soak so bright blood.

till my hands shackled like type,
score and more linked
mooring of a ship
ever gonna go.
orange
outmarled many ammonites

here are we
in the intricate paths of the stag
looking at it-death
his horns are in bars
his toes are split
away from the sticks he that can
see out

barely brick-red
a jay
calling like day
all the quad light to
slip and jut your restless head

oh girl
of fitting to my jettish ribs
(she) her mouth ope as a shell
staid on my spider hairs
all building

but then
do you know out?
rocking rivers, lorries
shitted earth corn
like a cat playing his brain, says
all the kids bent.
martyred at nothing.

the oiled smell of tomatoes
in nose
I been dealt well
topazy
day. my urine
's fine
sea-sidey. spilling in.

Cycle 4

(*On the Burning of York Minster*)

open-
ing

ove-
r BRIGHT WIND: BL-
ACK (WINDOWS) A DEC-
ADE. DOORS. JAMMD

all a night, noise
was as waves-concreted-to in travel
or made wake to an all-wall
walkt like leo
all the pile of stones –
the dog, dagger-fur. a stone-head, a biter
sharp on c'llapsing cans: comes
at raingagbow

all the learning lay
puzzlement: as their queen-bud and cow's tits

the statue . . . state of
gold! cuff! look here!

an' all the ships'ld come out on the sea . . .
fro' half-wall shelter,
the barques, and the mouthless ships
or the truck true
to track out the sun
                        at its lump of tangerine

pitch you with men:
to be a good pillow-maker
and match in black the feathers,
set up the lavender
to all and all the snub-nose Angles

what the brain put out
of outrage, arrogance
at animal or ranuncule
in towery arm, branched of, furcate

in the-leopard-the-tulip to
the dud gov^r and comp^a of the church of

the full seas
rains, splits
all the angel'd syllables (uncounted)
az bizarre in brachial flapping.
jurassic
bishop-pieces
looked sane, dead.

and in the gray lamps
or the leaves, merging grapeshot grass

at
flowers right-now
full az all foals (in its scouring)
oughta topple off their knees
at the glass around

quick qui'-violet burned exhibited

az mist made at its force
in the shift of steam
or in the chordal steam
                              (the rose roof-clouds)

by a vaulting of their rail-points, will-you
the lofty lozenge of the head;
tumbling (as dice) through the pólice-points
traced everything of their craniums
so mightn't forget it

so i walked where or covered
all its flooring such-wise – loops –
grated its height, in its shakey-sizes
(on ascension)

by when its noise, its its thunder
moved as in exaggeratedly
slow the steps
on
a hallowed a grotesque round

the grand bagged billy's eyes
strained out from the glass-indoors
at quaint manners of its ledding
an' loud earth-up

so that that lyric unease
as: sun near finished
itz track thru the zodiack

and the people, speaking, in spots
for a purple
shepherd
rao-rao-rao-rao!
– full or small, stiff-eared
limped, scritchy
scabbed-joint in his teeths

inside the work of the wall
in odd non-patterns
and lack of shine there

stutter and glum-
green, honing
but the chatter of fat heat
this fatter red to present in their piety
STUTTER AND GLUM-
GREEN, HONING
BUT THE CHATTER OF FAT HEAT
THIS FATTER RED
TO PRESENT IN THEIR PIETY

The shells and rockets from our ships

. . . .

several parties . . . admitted into the nave to view
                                        the spectacle

. . . .

only as tufts for
tooting at

Cycle 12

Oloi!
awry the
sun-spoon
dibbled & set up
little, smart be
beasty earth, you was weeding

as what trump?

on this sea-lion ticking & thinking keeping going,
   grey with grinning
demonstrate God and God's castle

i would plant it
seeing fish like plums
the penitent thief who got paradise ('an enclosed
   park')

wandering round walls &
shirking, you-bet
& i caught up in its
mock-monster, slagging, like on a rock-shelf
: would evade Canterbury, watching its waltz
eyes – a whitish

driving – lemon-looker
butterfly? in about bum
some wizards women take your tail too
The Sunshine-Hit-Back, New, Today, New Sun
Winding About The Shop Cleft And Cliff

go on

turn you
a spite wire cage
and do monkey-grope, round its square, or
gibbering like a glee, its grating

that is
that trigger off
man from man, rush back
 chases the soul from one to two to three

roaded, as if
Marenghi (at fair)
strange, up, cumb'rous
with wheel-side & what work her
not a war-rhythm no, not rhythm-war
and deep 'bone
ever' pipe be parted, wait, god-cornet

as South-
well dot sot
-ise (kirche-
schiff
Now whale-heads the world the
wall
     the trees and toes that
break the derivating, fields fold-up fallin'-to

shape shells chock of shells
white (whistled)
wiv salt, shaking
Like Swallows/Sea-Hearts SP-
Angle Blank / Crowdy
letterless
a lump-dry a flock-brain

a cocklesea

so the sands i saw
blooms a deep row, a blue bead
'plicated its budding

i stand maybe
i preacht the plant that –

in doubt about brain
bee, could be no bee (*Buzzaya!*) among the jungle

Hoo! Tug-horn
Tab
Lettuce-Smog

Archbishop Of A New Chess

let you wake up a bit and blow
Ever' Diamond Got A Red-Indi Top-Hat

are arrogant in their graves

as the politics of crab-baby, ashamed at its confusion

Hoo! hyam-horn
rescinds a note; go in
in-sombre

by breathing,
my head a flowerhead clicking with seeds
as vague as poppy-dead,   dog-puppet
and at the gold's note (she trumpets) love as
noddy-dream

new nor dead -spired -posed slop-shallow
learned burned broke at knee han'lumpy
dab grey grey-black b'slate sub-line sun
pass, pisses, titch bubble
love-splay, toucht. open as axe
a hoarse-hoard chest, a stale jail
and objects dyke grow would coll or cwm growl
rag thistle   i'wavy arms at war
out matrix   A to W   mocking the live (seashore)

matted and dead, you tread up thru foxglove forest-
    stems, git rifle, anyways
that waits and whines for when the saviour comes
with trumpet and trashing drums

leaning
with the style
i will shine the earth till it shines (gold-lion)

& plum grey cliff
                    that sun that walks
                                    disinterest

The Dance

It
iz
a
dance
(an oboe?
(a hunthorn?
a dart–over
ova text
an acrobat
ova text
the little ones
that make out act
and a trio, yes some
drum, drum,
step, step,
turn, turn,
jump, jump,
to duck that
to dip in dip out
while an olivewood huntsman
marks beat
in the closed pulse
as
there the jewels
sort
and sit
deep
and ground
and underground
in the chimneys
and tubes/spouts
in the sources
to high
overhead
in the rare cones

in the air
ARE
spas and flakes,
platforms,
links,
strange
rounding power
of sound
THEY FORM
some
up on an alp
sheep-balancers
by scant green
& top-grey crops
lime & stone,
screestone
lithe as shale
turned and shone
in a tumbling rock
and standing
hot with sun
or swaying
polished with wear
brown to ground
Or it is
a spill world!
they are our neck-nooses
a sport of courts
theirs, them, their shadows
are red
what is moulded up
as by some monsters
after their own way,
speck and spate
like if the sun shows fierce
we are always
shouting and burn

and if it is mild in show
we stand back
breathe
walk it round
to the circles
of creased lobes
and
In your cool garden
laden with stone
lidded with stone
still with earth-flowers
they
prefer to start to dance . . . .

Dog as Pirate

I turned up for apple-picking in a season there was no apples
come. That was the sort of pretence I know pretty universal.
I stood about a bit then hitched west. More west, the chalk
regains the sea. There are blue & other small chalklanders,
slight grasses & plants, unusual or usual. For the answer is
to withdraw your work, you will, anyway, soon be too ill
to continue it. The advent of water – as sea – the advent of
salt. Making extraordinary shapes. Sheep, and gulls and new
weeds. Fishermen (also anxious for grants); factories. From here
I commenced the business of wrecking, marking out the shore
with ranks/rows of animal-skulls and quarrelling over foreshore
rights and asserting copyright where I copied. The statements
I took and the techniques evolved for printing are appended,
somewhere. The gains – ghastly? – looked well by daylight –
green, brassish, crustiable . . .

Elizabeth

WHEAT BLU
      BLUFF
RAGGY EARTH; THE VISTA

AN CLAVIO-SUN (ASSOCIATE)
THERE, IS MOUSE AN' SNOW
SEE GO

EGG-SPLIT
WHAT A LAND-SPIT
SAND-BASED, LUNGS UP TALL, TROMBONAL
BRIDDIES CHANGING, AT SO MUCH MORNING

WHILE THE LAVENDER
IS WRESTLING
OR YOUR HAIR AVAILS
SING-SONGS, SEE-SAW

PAGINATION OF, LIGHT OF
BUFF PAVEMENT
OUT THIS DIAMOND

AND WE IS STILL
A PUZZLE OR

LO LOOK LO
AEROPLANE LITTLE CONE
AS SEA-KALE
WHOLE-EYE

METH-MAN THOU ART MY PAL
AND YOUR BOTTLE? AIR
OUR KINGDOM IN THE SKY, LOOKING
  LIKE GIANTESS' WEE

TURNS ITS RIBBONS – MARBLE THO
STRUCK DUMB IN THE MORNING
RIGHTEOUS (SOUNDING OF BOTTLES MADRIGALS)

FOR THE HOUSES
THE MALTA BLUE

BRIGHTON
WOUND A TOY
THE BEEFMEN COACH CAVALRY
YELLOW / RED

COMPLAINT OF A SNAIL
STOPPED LIKE A COIN END ON UPON THE EARTH
SHINY-SHOULDERED
TO THE SUN SAY
WHO MAKES AN ENGINE GO?

WHOLE CLOUD
CLAY GOLD
ALINER SMOKE
THIS HOST
AND QUADRILLION BRICKS
(LOVE)

LIKE TO LAUGH
CURVED LIKE FISHES (SHE)
SO A SEA COLLIDES
AMONG POUNDING, THE
EXPERTISE OF A BUTTERFLY OVER SURF
SEEKS A CENTRE

NOW CORFE;
TOTTERS
AT ITS LUMP AND SUMP
TOUCH AND CHURN THE RUBBISH
YOUR SMALL STERILE YELLOW LIMED BIRDS
WILL HAVE KIDS IN THEIR BEAKS BY YOU

WHAT SIGHTS WE SAW TODAY YOU AND I SYCORAX
  SAILING FROM POMPEY OUT
WITH THE LEVEL STEADY UNDERNEATH US
  MOVING DECK
OR ENDING NEAR GULLS
GETS GREY

DOT SPOT WATERFALL
MIZ ELIZ AIRY
CLUMPED   COLUMNAR
WEIGHT DAY-BIT

AFTER THE END THIS & THIS GOLD DAWN SAME NEW
SOME BALLING ABOUT THE SKY WAY VOLUMINOUS
ALREADY IS ENGINAL THIS WASHY BUM OF THE THAMES
SWAYS SKATES FIERCE FIREFUL LOVELY ALIGHT CRES-
CANT COLD SUDDEN AND SEA FRENZY PETES AND
THUMPS AS DRAGON POPPING AROUND HASPS HOLLOW
THE FINE THE RASPBERRY PLANT CONCLUSIVE

                    Grow
                    Break new
                    Thirstiest of chalk

                    And clear as charcoal
                    Sovereign

                    Sits still as an egg

                    Rolls like a wing-nut

                    Gonna catch it, start new blue, walk

                    But she went, as lucky
                    Oceanic and out of sight

The Festival

Wait! it's setting off. where? to what pattern? dunno. it didn't
have to be planned. any opportunity — something to be taken.

> Like in the can of the moon
> we are tumbled & tumbled around
> for fun.

In the city — no smoking, no fireworks, no dogs, no ballgames,
no work. heck! there's an awful lot to leave behind.

> Look! Solomon in all his glory
> never had an army
> as bloodily busy as our Queen's.

Who are they all? maybe someone's counted them properly. in
sheer reaction we seem to be

> More hidden than the unicorn
> more sky-full than the dragon
> trickier to tie than a triffid.

How can I be reassuring: there's no real way round it all but
movement.

> Listen, Alf, Pauline:
> it isn't you that has changed
> but the scene placed in.

It's what roads are for: to new places. people. signals. pleasures.
look what we've arrived in:

> A field of carnival
> set with moving
> tumbling brass, like bees.

East coast. one hour. sun on the field. two hours. cool, the blowing estuary, boatyards and estates. each place its own place.

> The buildings recognise it
> being low-set, modest.
> Long-Ears is the name of the Wind Dog.

> Every animal
> wakes
> and stretches.

> This is the Grey River.
> Like shot seed
> the wind-boats zip them' to and fro.

So we go on, house to house. possible. meeting the whole family. that is something – surviving even.

> Grave dancers
> jumpers, balancers
> on the world-top.

Completing the day. it oughted be something that rich. most, it is choked with rain, pips on the map, 'thorms' – thunderstorms. there are other things in mind:

> A night of the darkest blue animals
> of the deepest green boats
> tall wheels of darkened red.

Everyone takes for themselves, makes what they can. so why need for explanation? you know what's serious. like a boat-guard

> Over the swell from the boat
> if I see a wolf
> I will warn you with the sea-shepherd's rattle.

Five-Liners

The brush and tap of the twigs,
Things wind-rolled, then at a standstill
(The sounds we usually strain out)
The coming-up of an animal, a predator,
And outside, the monstrous approach and departure.

This man is wanted for questioning
Staring in/at photo
Do not let
Be sure to ring
And Dead or Alive

'Humane conditions'
The great grey blanks of sides
As long, as for ever, as a pyramid.
Matching the shifting, sliding sand,
Guarding the living body.

Let me pay a tribute to Isocracy.
It assumes
A system of equality
In which all the members
Are human beings. (but See Demonocracy)

All the rolls of pebbles
Are rhythms,
Excruciatingly complex patterns,
Of millions of years
Of training. A refrain.

A particularly lovely girl
Holding an orange tin.
Not what she looks like,
Or what she says,
But the voice, how it shines and tangs.

In the great light-chequered forest,
A party tracks our trees
And shoots them.
It is hard work for the hunters
Whose strange horns tangle in the dead wood.

What religion are you?
I offer him some farm cheddar cheese.
Perhaps my interrogator prefers unpasteurised goat?
In desperation,
I bring out the bright Stilton I got in Salisbury Market.

A goat
Riding on a dragon
And playing pipe:
A dance?
A carol. maybe.

When the Jesuit
Interrogated the shepherds
He asked how many Gods they recognised?
One of them knew at least a 100,
Another speculated 'About a thousand?'

Hatless
We stand in the snow.
Someone great is rumoured to be passing.
Sure enough, on the dot of twelve,
A New Year has arrived.

The plates of the boat are in the mud.
The wheel is in my hand.
What next, captain?
He checks carefully on the chart,
And we roll cigarettes.

The rules of school confuse the child.
I explain,
It doesn't matter.
The bus is late.
I wait in the disfigured town centre.

Oggi–oggi–oggi!
Shouting at the shower,
Screaming at the sleet,
Fucking under thunder.
Oi Oi Oi!

The teams spill onto the field
A flood of colour.
Gorgeous, exulting flame-brown colour.
All the patterns of football –
And in colour!

So what will you pay me for being good?
Good at lying?
Or loving?
Or lurching into work?
No, just generally, being good.

Flying in the door.
Flying in the light.
NO REWARD.
Flying out the light.
Flying out the door.

Just a smooth yellow sea
Flat in the sun
Quite, quite empty.
Sunny,
And bravely bright.

But the majesty of the WHOLE . . .
A chorus of heart-crossing work,
A great ball of feeling.
A maze of giant song.
Shining windows, and dust, and lots of drink.

End.
Why so much ink?
He is creative, of course.
Oh.
Get him to clean it up, will you?

Flower-Patch Units (1928) (*found text*)

1

a waving of reddy-brown tails / her big pink-and-white
erection / 'That will take some cleaning!' I said doubtfully.

2

The 'Orange King' and 'Lemon Queen' are great favourites
with us / yellowy-green and crimson / blackthorn / osier /
great charm of the East Coast Poppyland.

3

Patch was called up to receive a chocolate cat / unfortunately /
he found it was too big to be got through the door!

4

I've tried to count them, but they are uncountable / I wonder
what becomes of all the lost seed?

5

two lovely little sprites / lilting / give us a 'gardeny' feeling. /
But the gardener didn't end there.

6

I had suffered many things by reason of handy men who were
not handy, and gardeners who couldn't garden. / It actually
pains me to see the throw-outs lying pathetically on the bonfire.
/ I hate to deprive anything of life, so long as it is healthy and
harmless.

7

magnificent larches, towering spruces, Scots firs, Douglas
firs . . . great oaks, Spanish chestnuts, birch, ash, walnut,
lime and hazel . . . / I don't know how the air will hold
any more!

8

They proceed to do their toilet. / Baby didn't need showing
twice! / the whole estate – garden beds, orchards, fields, woods,
with the cottage itself

9

a gipsy / and / one swarthy gipsy woman / living up to the
character given them on the outside of the seed packet

10

the increase of ferns / giving a delicate ethereal look to the
leaves and flowers around them / this saves the expense / of
/ metal tops

11

Owing to the rapid thaw / gold and silver paper / was tearing
down the drive and leaping over the steps like a big waterfall /
'This is the brightest New Year's morning I've spent for many
a day.'

The GLC Abolished

Time to wake up again. The usual bears at the window. Could
the daylight too be growing?

> A solemn morning.
> The monster goats
> stir, in the out-fields.

> And in the day again
> Past the window, warm, and in
> the light plant-down shifts and stirs.

I am thinking of small things as I take breakfast, like any other
day. Suddenly to stop. As tho I had forgotten why I should
be uneasy. Or what sorts of foolery are afoot, with the smell
of discord.

> On the hills
> the wolves and foxes lie down and discuss
> what more the government can possibly do for them

It is as tho something is taken away from you, and the thief
returns to punish you for carelessly losing it. What can you say?
Yet there is something more than just grotesque about this day;
it is self-defeating:

> The mouth of the dragon
> twists
> to bite its own tail.

For today, the government will make a city disappear. No more
London, not even a shire to take its place! I open the windows
of my friends' flat to watch the transformation, uncertain what
is happening.

Exhilarating?
over the plants,
the mountain range.

In the width of windows
viewing the warm brick
the sides of the mountains.

There the houses
are folded and waved
in a complex of mountains.

The wall that is faces of houses
is plain and square: such brick
in new mountain-building.

Curves keystoned,
brick arches in roman threes
like mountains, ancient, again.

present as a curtain wall
that are cliffs
and ridges

And at night
the lights are here then there
in the caves of the face.

Gold Found Texts

all different things that had been built running thru this is may
it please God it aint just a silly dream while I'm in here venture
proclaim their intentions it is impossible that there will not be
some good lands found I love you I've always loved you and
always will love you. I love you. love you. I love you. try suss it
all out. made me. happy. come Manoa and El Dorado and many
other provinces. they all say, they can't keep me forever.

went to work. so I can brighten up. shells and beads, salt and
dogs, well my love, as you can see I've arrived, us not making it,
jaguar skins and birds they call caharos, this concealed province,
now I can wind up that sloppy jock next door, decorated 'em,
one day, cinnamon of the most perfect kind, you captured it, I
ain't gonna take, does God think that because it is raining, across
specimens of gold, I'm not going to, these scarecrows, no shit
off of no one

Well babe. how are you babe I'm bloody shattered. cannibal
and warlike. bellicose people. started off a right bummer. very
embellished with poison. slide back. a bowl about a foot wide.
everytime I put an application in. great tricks. they fuck it up.
in conformity. my diamond. I give up on this fag. aspirin water.
no fertile or abundant province. I can't even keep a fag alight.
on account of the roughness of the country. this dump. I'm
gutted. or he'll send the letter back to you. no I'm not allowed.
I have to buy all that.

a break. a lump of stuff they call cake. shitpit. biting his hands.
ordered. all their treasure. but good appearance. thrown into
the lake. things of little value. take everything else. low today.
off you. banged up. read books. until whatever. wish they still
put the white stuff in the tea. really helps the time. didn't know
I'd written as many letters as 38. the golden man. I'll start on
me cake in a minute. according to labour. a steel ball with
movable claws. rooting about in my mouth. reckons I'm a

gannet. picture a lovely autumnal day. legend. roll myself a
smoke, relax. in this joint. at its bottom

★

its quiet and bloody cold. that great lord or prince goes about
continually. I can dream. can't. I. to put on armour plates.
that ain't a bad idea. about being thrown about a bit. plates
of hammered or stamped gold. covered in gold dust. if this
desperado gets back up on the fence. found. this geezer. about
covered in gold dust. arms. slashed up. no other clothing. no
impediment or hindrance. since I've seen it. clothed in that way.
like the state of his arms. on top of it. the blood. less beautiful.
its stuck in my mind. when I try to. fine as ground salt. close
my eyes. discarded and lost. unusual. more costly. there, the
blade, the blood. natural form. to powder oneself with gold.
stuck. thoughts that were running thru my head. I was laying
in the sand. I've gotta squeeze out. clothed and covered.

★

on dark nights / these rings / a dragon began to rule / getting
£15, £18, £20 / hoard on the high heath / supposed to be gold,
we tried a funfair first, cldn't sell any / some kind of man
entered there / a restaurant, the guy says it's worth £20 /
approached close to the treasure / to sell them quick, they
have hallmarks and everything / the hand / go black on your
knuckles / took a cup, large and gemmed / golden rings with 3
diamonds in them, they cost more / when the dragon woke he
didn't disguise the fact / you had to carry a tin of brasso round
with you / that he had been tricked by a thief

★

Our attention now turns to the small family group that, at an
early date, must have worked into the valley. The Valley with
its side branches was of considerable size, black and white, tan
and white, piles of sand and rock, recognisable, a small herd of
goats, a container full of wheat kernels, and garlic, leeks, and
onions in branches. His men, a recumbent jackal, uncovered
a step cut in the rock-floor of the Valley. For their own food
supply the lively animals doubtless secured a scanty living
from the river plants, trenches, the wheat scattered in shallow

furrows, and warrens. By the next day they had uncovered
twelve steps revealing the upper part of a doorway, numerous
passages connecting 'chambers' inhabited by individual families.
Once well established, additional items of food were the birds'
eggs taken from nests in the reeds. Beyond lay a sloping tunnel,
two or more entrances, so that if an enemy comes in, till thirty
feet along the tunnel was a second doorway. The lives of the
men and women went on pleasantly and serenely. Then came a
great discovery. If the goats were – 'Can you see anything?' 'Yes
wonderful things.' For such a mild emergency, mist, strange
animals, statues and gold – I was struck dumb! – everywhere!
the glint of gold ————————

Hammer Poem

wild
up hair
grass
the pebbles play
stammer on themselves
loop beast-shapes
Hey! whe'
whazza sight now?
All I nee'
i –
iz
Roa(d) long
who nee(d)z where
not my concern

Harrow

In this muck's city
A host
A HOST OF
With the bells (and bells)
View of a dimnshed church
I got out

But the world doesn't want buildings
Or us, seaside folk
Or our dead.

Now it is, the sun burns
And the earth / flowers crack / break
With bones. Beardless
Bodies are give up
That were good too.

For accidents, the pin-man, I'm down and iron.

Such
The rain comes down a heck
That the totters can't catch it that fast
Or their clouds race about the sky
And I get freshness, out it
As I had never done naught
(To tear the wet stones down of the castle)

The Hawksmoor Mausoleum

I

Can cities have health?
and, are they surer places?
Bridges –
where? and for who?
silent, empty, in sequence.

2

A great rotunda
of balancing,
of balanced drums
(performances).
curved
ribbed
as the horn of a ram
almost part of the land.

3

Ravenna, certainly,
is evoked,
and
Theodoric,
the stones
drawn ready around.
Who lives in this shiny circling house?
Why, it is empty!
A hollow,
A resonant
Land I walk on.

4

Through the fibres of the park
I took this snow-way and that.
My breath whited and greyed, varied.

Petrified,
defensive,
intensely smoky,
it is as a balancer of fog –
cold air / cold sea
so the jewel, the crown
dissolve

5

Pages as
better records as regards
the hides of goats
than lime
or brown tile?
Or will any of it?
Such at
the leap
ova calf.

6

This one
speaks of the same time-tumble too.
Others
stars suns storms.
A torrential land
like glasses tuned and sharded.

7

Consider the landscape.
and the way of construction of them.
Probably
the daughter of the cuckoo king
– the niece of the invisible ones –
chose it so.
Now

because it is fearful
the land.

8

The stone rhymes
limps
reads.
But a breeze
– the season is such –
the sea keeps turning and turning upon itself
itiz a sort of drying drum.

9

But making
pure sound?
Imagine
        continuing as sound!

10

So high
in the house
only the birds' wings' sounds . . . .

11

The strange site
sight of circular rails.
Here
there
a little cretin or Christian
or a land–holder
a dance he is forming out.

12

'Fraid, scaring humans
excavated

from a million cells
or sheds. How ill we are held.

13

Now, because it is fearful,
the Land.
With farts and churned feet
Six gaunt-hipped cattle fill
the grey field,
forked and clear spiteful.

14

The throb
of great
water-beasts
travels
the fair.

15

Adios
sez the
sun boat structure
before the blue rock.

16

The county is a gross shell,
you walk on it
you bounce you bowl on it
like a gigantic burp
and the Passage
is un–
jovial.

17

Transit

18

Look again
at the land
how parentless
complex complete grown and ordinary.

19

In the zone of confinement
the boy fisher
the glass jar
and the djinn.
in that stark and surly round ova place
the body is dumb
the teeth
move in the mouth.

20

Now now
I will balance you, out
just on the
shelves of my shoulders.

The House

Bit drunk the potter
boots in his own door
YOU POTS he shouts
why are you all and one
i-den-teek?
why are you everyone
exact alike; and FLAWED?
what's more
he set about his job
and so they got broke.
at sun-up
he swept 'em out –
no shards in my shop!
See –
they are the sparks
of the bones of larks.
take the clean bone soul
of a dog
the fluter is no one
can't see
flower-size
root-ways
there-through
Now
what bright bricks!
clear rooms!
garden!
it all seemed so
easy there
only too
that same easiness
he said
that's
bringing them up
attached

like
for totting up
as last year
I give-give
four palms
20 fingers
like a hedgehog
and let distribute them they.
laid out
left aside
the pockitid
seeds off
of balsam
zip and zip
are
triggers some
rockets
and fire ash
more and
here the chest will arch
the spine rise nearly, it is
what blocks the shoulders
up to width and strength
like how I grow
and the air
busy
between the shoulders, shrugs –
what a level, even place it is
these targets!
but the useful
citizens!
like some
today
exculpates
(in anything)
and the yards
and squared rooms

thinking
like the wires in a watch
When the new house
was achieved
what bright bricks!
clear rooms!
garden!
it all seemed so
strange there
only too that same newness
was pleasing
to see
and every plant
began
to cast its
ropes up
with a joke . . .

Industry & Idleness (*The Hogarth Prints*)

1. work is one, how does the sun
pipe an' mug, & book fun
turn itz spindle like on a law
or I like sleep's see-saw
Any taut Christian spy
is welcome by

2. as I ought, owe Chance
as how the coins dance
under my hat
like that
Sunday's man, skull, needs his watering-can

3. Mum and Dad and my kid-Cat
gonna hang me near as that.
sail, pump-sail and the waves hey! rail on about
I wanna shit out
you're only wood, not god?

7. be on shore
or wow I whore
so no one bust in but me; jumpy? like my whole cat
in her Fat

8. getting all this and Scrip'
and no ship
Look at that gold: tubby turnip
as the kiddies
trundle by shouting Look out it's manacles
me earning on, get shooting?
when the Watch come tooting

10. sir, don't wince
you're! a real prince!
an' I reckon this must be the end
amen

11. this is the last dying speech & Confession etc. won't it make Xmas weather!

12. a full and true account etc.
(good ink) ghost of etc.

On Insurance

Trilobites occurt
as litt'e balloons in 'e rock

Roads:
Suffusions of sweaty hearts.

In some valleys
White huntsmen at the break of day
riding to wooden beds in the ground, shouting.

Seats for twenty or maybe 25 gods: like
Gog, Marylebone, Bees, Ironbridge,
Albion, Amyl Nitrate, Devil's Island, Wembley . . .
Dead minds to 90%; ours almost crippled

Sweating so severe
for trees

Be in a field
Part of me, like   an hare
Cavorted clear
And like an old maid some of it
Stayed with hips aching

Most of the environment *is* locks.
A lock about Sea Rocket as big as a toilet door.
A roof over the Umbelliferae as tight as a baby's pram.
And when they lock, they block.

Brass tablets
And stone basalts, truths on them

Sly Street
Seven Star Alley
Christian Street
Cinnamon Street

Lemons,
LORRIES,
defoliation, a parcel:
2oz. gorse + 4oz. sandstone

This royal arrangement, this satisfactory sequence, the terrific
    testicles, sometimes wincing and telescoping up.

The small ears
of the grass flamed white, crimson

Message to be tapped into space like: $1_1 + 1_2$

Interruptions

In a blue bowl
basalt and white
the eggs / the clouds
comic cones of ice
sinwalt – affording no entering . . .

So heavy a work
it rushes
bangs up over the head
makes dizzy,
jangles, grows
crescate, never getting . . .

A bar of chrome,
a tint, a paint,
slender, broaching glow,
warm away:
not a lock, a couple
so solid it fades . . .

A cloth of water-chicks
doubling and crossing
they have lines and they hoot
being young, too loud
like for ever
(along, along . . .

I work the alphabet:
pictures that explain
or in neatness fur and refuse . . .

A sight ov incompleteness / interruption . . .

A fantasy door
silver-vein'd
almost a shameless cheer
that it two-heads in & out
with colossal change . . .

Just at the turn ov sleep
that moment (a hesitation)
a heart-pause, a crinkle or sigh
ere I roll down . . .

On the Involuntary Muscles

Great sunlike unsober field of
milk-shadows, men and war-walls
unsteadied and
all panning one way
eroded, silent, wry-tacking, servantile,
leading the child like a loop-serpent
to the sea-point and spray
key-traced, corneted and opaque, mild blue /
blind yllow
moving and not making, moving.

To Johnny Prez Hells Angels Nomads

1. Christmas straight–
Jacket kid
Packet of light fields
Eye
2. With no lamps, roads
Without airforce or Angels, wd you jin Ruislip?
A lion in you
In a law-shop
3. The motor-bike is acorn yellow
Johnny Bev Bob
White my mind
Gonna pick up of
Pepper is day yep
4. Bev as the sea wave wake
See this this is Angels getting the booting of their life
   in Scrubs
This is Johnny
This is me picking up snout bits in Brixton
5. Johnny begot, beading of black Jack-club
Dance kick at drums, can-banging
Death–douce
6. And love
Works to mix you up miscates the soul
Love
Shooting blood out; all
Red-laking; well
Shut in the breasts of her.
7. One of a group of blokes like zoo-bears
Hill-less and wall-less were
Underanimally fighting back
And gets busted
New
8. In the morning, Hate rose, very red,
Like the head of the fucking sky, bright

And public, warning
Morning broke out
(Not anxious, eager, but slowly, really serious)
9. Alone   All
10. Free   Awaiting
11. The yellin sun
(For Aries' person is red-glad)
Rides and roars bike
Summer street
12. Stood with my hands for an hour
From the edge
(Are you tired yet
said the dtective?)
13. Johnny setted
Like land, land.
Castles and Corn and Clouds and Courts.

On the Jurassic

I saw wrote up
'do not display, play'. I saw a ————.
. . . I see lots of metals

A smell of plants
where the streams run out from rock

Sea licks my breast
many many patterns of
millions – which is also all the plant tips

Talking Cycads
volv-ed loop a lithe tree

The finger is not shy of the nostril
the palm is not shy of the arch
the bone of the back is not air-wary

From the sand:
gold plate clutter and litter almost
against it
an unfolding grace of-a-spider.

'Listen' I say:
'All your increasing Beauty
will be star-exploded off the planet

'Look at the geology of getting to die: it radiates out from
points of repulse, layers forth, agglomerates or finds rings of
extra danger . . .'

After the argument
great patterns of little bronze pins above
encrystaled and slipped
by my head

the oldest land is gleaming too
as a silvery show
for miles each way

comes as high tremor
of morning
when almost all
the last
fragment of obvious heat
h'evaporated off of earth
and my blood too
as cold as that is

Kinderscenen

1.

When we awoke (the morning) – now there was no city
around us! Only, softly and evenly, leise u. sehr egal, ash,
tipping and lilting, mounting with sad sound (in klagenden
Ton), bespread the whole view, with one or two people and
things still moving through like very bad and exaggerating
horsemen. 'Lo! Morgenwanderer!' they called to us, 'where has
the bread-shop gone to in all this?'

2.

Into the land of tigers! frisch u. kräftig, frisch u. munter, frisch
u. fröhlich, munter u. straff. Orange and wax-white, orange
and amber under, with rotting jaws. It was strange, so strange,
the manners and land-talk, frequent fighting, the funereal sort
of the jokes, immer schwächer. Zart! Soon it is our meal-time.

3.

A landsman, girt on him like a yoke, a butterfly of enormous
wings ~ so he is quite unable to work! Reapers here, moving
in line, and before them there are clouds of butterflies ~ all a
protein-yellow colour like the wheat ~ rising from the wheat.
On a battlefield when horsemen have to have a piss, grey &
sober butterflies settle in their clothing. They are as thick on
the ground as mottoes and wise saws.

Latchmere (*Remand*)

Notice it notice (eyes, eye, ear)
Spic' of wheat
the buds-brown, brutalised, at their gate out the state

sub jugum
            in wolf-vault
in the gardens of Poknies and po-lice
coplines   teacher; breach
tongues out
mouths up clovery windows
Latchmere
solitary – no – lead-lifting
tongue
tight as tap

fuse your fucking heads

low slow river-weight
many-ribbing multi-Keaton
my alibi

laugh what laugh marmalade, gentle like pus
swimming this quiet
patch-maze; swims and
speeds-up

Leeds, Kirkstall, Staithes

The city: dust, lots of dust about it, through it.
I buy a bright orange-yellow balloon there.

An abbey: unrebuilt. The cloisters
must have been of wood.

There is wet on the floor: but it were not much work to bring
    it again
to the humiliation of the humble and the engrossment of the
    proud. Who would pay for it?

It is Spring: with flowers bright as carrots.
and a dog white head on little pole.

A potash mine: it is in the key of A.
A scale of A, A, A, A, A, A, A, A, (without intervals)

A furry mineral.
The room has skulls with it, and bald hematite.

The mines extend under the house,
is all about high fatalities,
And their relationship to high unemployment.
In 1977, there are white clouds and sky everywhere.

The southwards heaths are a very rich and brown
    ruddy colour.
From the sea edge they spiral in, are reforested, make me dizzy
    (like a parasite)

Angles and squares in the building:
On the beach the shapes are not so different.

Window or lozenge. Primroses, lambs, seaweeds,
cows, next fossil fish, grasses, jelly limpets, all in shape:

What I cannot make out,
Are they signs of life then?

What all the calendars are like,
And the pages full of.

In the climax to the abbey, dogs leap about.
Rain shower. Three children shoot a rugby ball through
    the window.

Then go away. I get the sums right?
It is in the form of a long arcade.

Long Elephant Song

Once the world was full of these more giant
sizes, now smaller and smaller
till the weakest germ even
will be undersea.
There will be zoos and time will be
forced backwards. Mountains being fenced off.
And probably sixty elephants.
Blue whales separated for ever from old elms.
ONCE the world separated for ever from minute
    animals
then smaller and smaller
even the weakest elephants will be
old. Now blue whales of more giant sizes
forced backwards, being fenced off.
Mountains and sixty giants will be there.
Elm's germ was wished first and
creating full undersea
Till these will probably be time-zoos.
ONCE these smaller and smaller elephants
even the mountain's sixty weakest sizes
will be giant, undersea.
Was world full for ever of separated creating,
Blue germ and minute time
will be whales, giants there
from old animals being forced backwards
now the more fenced off.
Elms and zoos, probably first wished, will be
    till then.
TILL once the zoo's world was giant and germ,
Mountains and minute, elephants, elms,
old, smaller, smaller, weakest, fenced backwards,
    form . . .
whales, giants of sixty sizes, will be creating,
    forced:
for ever-time,

the more beings will be separated
even off these animals – now
blue undersea

Magistrate

First the magistrate put up the kid face to death
Hey, Blue! Tell?
What cars a'like racin' at you
Have you seen morning yet, midday?
Dying is Azazello, he aint a friend nor.
Namore.

Mandrake Song

who, obscene hey?

you're in my fairground yep

I bawl
about
about about by my navel

I oped
Both Eyes

it groweth in the greas
ov dangled men

an' I threaded my boots up

bawls about about
the bottles, caps. billionz

so I set the room
with white, with great garlic
ty-in' the white spikes in cotton

but this's the beach?
stones? are clouds, is it, them?
solemn, son! smooth:
difficulty w/ the glass here.
leave the window. at the door

so there's some tight snag
a megalithic maths
got me there

not today, no, not-like, not today

cos it screams
scratches
like babe's brain bowl

you think you're, only, lucky?

Mark's Slide

Arriving at Arkengarthfell
  a play so perfect
    rose sun on taller parts
      opposite, the sheer stone rounds
        of the hills' ridge
          wildened to redcurrant
          over the ruin-sheds
            Mark would like to live in
            and the concept of it
              grew its snail round and round
              to the full.

Moorsrider

Plumstones by the
hotel porch –
It has four pillars.

Are the days, days
of the cornfield
wasted?
Are the bricks of the sea
vacant?
Skelton and Stanghow
are lovely.

Pepper-coated cows
at their grazing
behind furze.

There was
the word CAUTION,
a picture
of a lamb frisking.
Later a
sheep
inside a red triangle,
and the fields were ditched and crossed
and spotted with baby goats
biding meek enough by,
hoofs sliding in
bluey-pink heather bells.

Once
Sixteen Gods
in a violent show-down
smashed up the landscape.
Still the dark bones can
quarrel spectacularly
across the dale.

Six, seven firemen
taking a picnic
there while their larger engine pumped in water,
and rolling about.

Lime people
live here.
Their sheep
are used as milestones.

Who ever thought
of joining the fields up with walls?

The fog has blocked up the valley.
Glaciers were like it once, truly
and ground the land out
thoughtless and thorough,
scooping
(without rime or reason)

The sheep
almost climb in the car-boots
for food.
This is the prairie edge.

Thru the dry streams
I come to the minster.
(It is made for St Gregory)
though he has now died
and indeed anyone else who might have been here.

The minster, Orm's work,
is a muted place,
place of half-worked stone
and plain or missable
ornament.
Tostig figures in the superscript
who killed Orm's father
and
with appropriate guilelessness
he left the names in juxtaposition for ever.

When I walk
there is not much to write about.
Seldom are there any discouraging words.
Excepting landowners'.
But their hearts are cruddier, less cute
by not sharing.

Sweet and taut
this long extending roof of moorland
lies like in a grave sleep:
parts are bracken green
parts, plain dream,
laps and pools of dark-dyed land
folding
at waves and rides

By the driven storm
boxes of Transylvania
come recklessly close.
Probably the lifeboats
bearing deadmen's names
assist them in.

The last landmark
is Wade's Stone.
It stands in a farmfield
and the sea and the sun
rising and falling
set and move on either side
as frictionless markers in a meshing cognisation
of perpetual, perultimately largo
melody
composed by Wade, son of Weland.
Good night.

Moving

Little home, we're on the move again,
Romany now, a Chal
we're jalling akadi Mark's orchard
be'it yellow, be'it red,
filled with apple-suns and
biscuit-tins,
grass & bicycles,
flower-workers and long-ears
whistling the by-laws as they piss.

Nativity

like mine
moth'd rust-up
bootz,
buttonz on my khaki jeans, yep
Iyama shepherd: She agrees

they, they's eyes, yo! they
millionz of summery eyes
sow'd az a tapioca most
'at curds-up or cuts in the tabby sky
so it's such turmoil

(I cut the pieces out too)
whe'we went into the town
w/ 'e sheep wandering on like at criss-cross(
drinkin' an')
looking for the cam'ras

November

Migne's printing
of Bede's *Mensium Notæ*
has a November wood-cut:
a bumpy field is shin-deep with snow
a short-cloaked traveller is caught in the open
between two solid-ink dogs.
He has his spear at the jaw of one
while the other attacks him from
behind and his hat has already tumbled off.
Near the row of trees in the background
someone is walking along with a stick
and someone is creeping up on him with a cudgel.

Thus,
caught between the Ice and the Ice Maiden.

danger,
continual, irremedial anger
in the creeks and viks of the stars
in the cool-way day-time

sky-scratches, day-swings
it is an open harvest of foundlings and demons

late and vast spiders yet spun
stained glass
over
and over and in the arcades
waterhorses slip and jeer with day-fulls of complaints

equally the filth of beetles
and the cochineal in the chalice,
matches of lions
and air-circles of dragons, the pomp of it!

we have killed
or badly injured a multitude of plants
(says Darwin)

it is autumn certainly
little presses are pegged up to dry to be packed away.

do your feet meet?
are your ears near?
do your eyes di-verge?
are your soles whole?
oh do your fingers sing?

I am storing fifty-one seeds of Goatsbeard:
so I can sow again.
Now I have lost them. Now I search again.

Nut's Small Poems

In the house where I break the gate
into
six-sided nuts,
slate-bright and chapped. And grow up.

Beechnuts,
a wood box for each,
a label, 'hollow'
they are scattered in millions,
I like them like
brass, brown as gold.
It is time to shout.

The fire fox must cross the great frozen water,
with a snack nut in his maw,
it will be worth while to cross the great water.
Later he is cheated of the nut, tears the flowers up and
Bites. Publish.

This group of nuts wish
anonymity.
They are not a gift from me,
or to me.
I ask, one by one,
till they answer, I am not afraid to die, I am afraid
to die, I am afraid to die, I am not
afraid to die, variously.

The scotcher of laughter
makes a flood of nut-drops
fall of goddess' white lid-wood of her lashes
onto her lap. There is no laughter.

These are tall walls
with nutmeg shipped in, in a dense-polished bowl of brickwork
Also, darkness, with
egg-blobs, cased away, when her
end shone as a wide nub, Can you see?

banged up at
church tower –
that was sprinkled with white flints
over
head, scatter,
that even chalk makes nuts there, glint-nuts
I saw near, like
prisms, so Iris. Distribute.

They are ubiquity, overproduction, procreation.

Outre-mer

A chain of littled circumstances
From my scored thumb
To the sugar-tub – This is the way
The line
Marks itself (para, s'tence)

In its directions: like from dead start
When the Sun in the sea turned to brown
And blew to dust – left to stand,
Its puzzled way
To Outre-mer

Where the riders sealed their heads,
Dead, bled,
This company – with hawsers for hands
And spoke like locks,
Thrashing and calling their way.

Based in the amber place of the soil,
And the living threads
Worked loose – sending out, backing
Their damage
In the dark.

Calling the worship of the Lady Lark:
The tap, the panes of light,
Pristine and sativate – smeared
With globes of in-colour,
Bobs and pig'radiance.

These that are curved
Mauvelettes of wood
Know which way the credit works – too cute
To contribute, too wary
In the wreck, the debt, the repeated whims.

The swiped reject band,
Too sure of it,
Too busy – only caught
To the bumpless sunscape,
The rough of furze, rhododendron too.

'As there I was
Riding along on the back of my dinosaur
And the waves housing up – And
Concentrating onto my wet feet
(I had to think of something to stop being sick).'

The lean and taut sheets of the body,
Damped with work,
Over-sweet – With the strange
Eye-tricking balance,
The spread of the wrestler.

'So there, and bright
Coming by down
On the bikes – till the bars locked
And shot us headover in the ditch,
So shattered as we laughed outright.'

In the far, smoothed-high province of the Jutes,
The coil of a mirthless sky,
Open, cogent, fair – and its buried
Purchase/energy, bare and careless
Working a way thru the strawberryfield.

Paracycle

This dawn this, dawn
Not unlikely
a reversal of its day's end

It is pale glass
meets my fingers up
from the floor

You are going to wash that
You and your new pals

Are going to wash that
and maybe
a no-beat day and an easy day

That one slamming one bloke into the wall,
And me, he says, knows me?
Me?
Who spawned this fucking day?

Got I walk.
Watch them searching us out.
It's people weeing everywhere, I would reckon.

Almost he thinks of hymns.

Now at seven, maybe,
let the kids out.
give them one or two of toast an' a beaker of tea.

Mornings they come to me screaming
Or smiling.

One or two dogs come with us to school.
This way, the lollipop lady won't cross with them.
It isn't Alf or me is their Dad:
Only Pauline belongs to them.

Alf threats them a flat whack with a bit of plastic track.
Or maybe it's me. They will fall down.
They whine for money.
They are frightened we will run away on them.

No grudges.
If I get you today, no grudges.
So I don't look at it as living on a planet:
more, adding up of chances.

Someone is bound to start banging at the pipes.
I reckon, that and shouting. (It figures,
It dawns on me.)

★

Only to have been on report.
After pulse
It rushes my throat,
literally, like terror.

He behind the desk
As the joke-wender
Says why don't I leave the country?

It is very slick as:
It didn't happen to me, now.

(And what is my work?
I don't know that)

But it may do.

You were just walking down the street they stopped you?

Almost for despair he shouts
Was it this way?

No no no no no no no no
No no no no no: what the fuck is that to me?

What facts was I collecting?
What on earth worth?

No, I have nothing to complain of.
Yes, there are things to complain of
But no, I have nothing to complain of

Or I mean, I have no way of complaining

Except
Of what I done.
Maybe we could fix it
For you to admit to
That one. You see . . .

The servants of the servants of Set
will not look at your malice.

*

Already early already the sky flat-chest-ribs:
White kitchenful of new things.

Between us
A new magic solar zodiac –
No great wove
Waiting breath.

Says she nothing of its ice-golds.

I mean, will I ever make this
Anything like living to?
Like?

Sometimes of its own accord
it becomes rawd hands like burnt brix. corn,
patienter than the planet down.

How the day dives
not in my diet now,
nor no dawn, where the
oil-ships grab out the blue rind of the seal from the white.

*

What got evening now
But only Gargoyles? No way
jocular now, a crude new garrison
of ungames.

By Post Office and Sidney Square drains
in the May heat, that complete stench,
is dark, strong.

Only what fat heads
Park them in the dark top
so as to make me up
some tiny A-rab

Turning into any line of words
Dont't know,
What I can't reckon up, so much darkness for anyone.
And gritted against their Dad.

Unbuckle jeans for bed
Unbuild the clothing, com-
pounding mind (is it)
again
Against

Where's the scalding cold
at my arm my lung
lamp to the whip-tricks
of Air/August

*

This house:
ants.

One week,
A thunderstorm
from the direction of the docks.

Tonight, near:
Full-grown?

*

Nearby, this bridge:
crash-work.

Like to
Been of broke ankle
On a site of fresh battle,
with the crows there

Or
by brittle licked ferns an'
a almost perspex-sight water

Work for big rollers
to tar and level out.

Few houses, upright.
Bric-brac, them.

For example,
dead.

I am waiting for allthings to sort themselves out.
like a phonecall,
to go abroad.

An invocation, then.

No one of them unnecessary.
Not Alf, nor Pauline, nor me.
Dissatisfied the objects of government gotta be.

Grizzled toes, or
popped arms.
Jacket, jacket with seagull badge pinned on.

Video box on.
Spare transistors in three jars on
my shelf,
maybe three amplifiers.
I can only explain the fan-heater to Graham.
The whole area
so much,
Looks smashed, mangled, by base of sky
In the same rising, remember?

Pattern-Peeps

cute eight yellow-lions
biscuit-edged on the petals
outstanding the song of hum of interference

so to cross water
the Ninja if he shows himself
gums on leaves (skin-scales)
walks on wood-shoes over the river-top.
Look, like a word, he isn't visible.

the turquoise sugar-stain,
the yellow eyes:
toads, adders, spike-newts
spell out local adverts, in nature-breaks

AMERICA
discovers itself
to be homosexual!
with little pockets
of
bisexuality

There are flaring blue cups of coal
deep streamers of mauve
in the diesel

Turn the wires:
there are great laid-dryer fields of brix
burning redder,
shifts, tans, 'sort of super-carrot'

Droitly the whale-hunter
weighs the focus
& centres on
a snowflake

Everything moves into pattern
like words in poetry
(tho few enuf stay there)

It switches /
buttons flash /
there is the unmistakable odour of authority
& cheap silver forks

death spinel –
flack.
The great cake of the city endensens itself.

And we dodge,
dodge
and the pinball track
and the cellotape-trumpet-board rounds/hems it all
    so lovely

Review

I had never seen so many stars.
It was a cause of astonishment.

★

These trucks were ready loaded for the morning and watched.

★

Even on the first day when all the water made like a wrapping
of blue rock (utterly steady), the sun rose on, obliquely showing
in grey from above in all white, with impacted engines, unseen
not turning, new unpainted

★

The snapdragon that would not be picked
The dog caught in trusting its master,
Coloured petals, the prize of the whole
Garden, And some are white, some red, purple-with-white,
   and black and white

★

And I reckoned yes I reckoned I could see the exact spinning
   of it

★

There was a dragon for the great south-heat, and a dragon
   for the ice

★

Civilization is our cogwheel doric and chamfret – do not
   dare overset

★

It is to be
'Never asleep'. And
'All all the Tomorrows

*

Michael collected up all the ducks from the county. – If you do not help me, he said to God, I will kill these ducks and I will kill these ducks until you help me. Later the police came and stopped him – we are coming they said. But those are no hostages they said, it's just something maniacal.

Rondelle

Regarding wall-flower
Umberish or cork-colour
half-loose happy
half-tight sort-toasted like it has shoulders
Sand-regard
has bright-burns
close to – giant & tarry
Regarding

Sea Shanties

1.

Locked in in the beauty,
Locked into the beauty,
Locked in in the beauty.

2.

Swelling, the sea-swell
At the tape of the boat, tapping,
And turning, a tower of noise.

3.

Blundering, to be blunt about it,
In the darkest bits of the canal, night-bound,
Bound into a blind alley

4.

Fishing, the night fishermen
Set out houses of lighted floats, bright floats,
Bobbing in the black.

5.

Stinking, the trumpet of daylight
Sets us moving, on the motor,
Rocking thru the locks, thru London.

6.

Lounging, at one lock,
I buy a twister, a fish-lure, big as a fish-fist,
From a kid, out the cut.

7.

Galloping goats, above the boat,
Tall, horned, & ibex-like, behind tall wires,
And opposite, an opera-cage of – birds!

8.

Shouting, when I show the map.
Because of the routes you can take out, the choice
    of out-routes,
Vowing that it has to be Bow Locks.

9.

Riding in the dire lull of Bow Top.
Taking a moment to sleep, a minute of sleep,
Tiring, in the high level lone-place, for the tide.

10.

And poised below, tide-side of Bow,
On the pulling, pouring tide, feeling its flood,
Able-anxious to accept it, with the lights set.

11.

Banging, the boat leapt out,
On its treacherous little motor, magically mute,
A scary shooting-down, how to stop?

12.

Tugging at the tuft-stems of these slope-plants,
I try to arrest, rest our pace,
Startled, and with a smacking sound, they start from the
    wall, rootless.

13.

In the black cocoa of Bow Creek,
the pudding-masters take a thick streak,
striping, and brand the bow.

14.

Re-powered, a power-run down Bow Creek,
Right, with the steering working, having steerage,
Overcoming the canyon, out to the broadest ways.

15.

Parading, thru the pride of Greenwich,
Choosing a gate thru the Barrier, how grand a gateway, and
Stunningly, no one stops us.

16.

Tumbling to trouble!
Now we lose way again, again in the reaches, unpowered:
Making a poor mazurka, round and slow round. Which way?

17.

Seeking to see the true Thames channel,
Now at night, pylons light & line it, tall pyres of bulbs,
Branding the banks out, as it swings erratically.

18.

Listen – the slight sombre showing-up of day
And the massed furniture of docks, half-missed
As slowing, we go down past Canvey.

19.

Standing stranded
The long Southend Pier, long & strong,
Embedded with the bulk of a smashed wreck, on its east.

20.

Chopping, the choppy waters of the mouth
As we make the estuary out, out to the wider water,
And the blaring blasting tankers and mountainous wake.

21.

Anchoring, letting the anchor out
Shallowish the sea but hard to see
Clouded with the same clouds us a sub-blue sky.

22.

Waking in the way of the tide
Now we ride on a cascading sea, deep and then high,
Tumbling about, in this tumble who will bring the
    anchor onboard?

23.

Calming, to a sweet calm sea,
It seems safer a lot, here by the Maplins, ever evener,
Steadying, we are steady now on the bottom, stuck.

24.

Gliding away from the gilded sand,
Now the tide has left us to wait, watch for the new water,
Stranded on the large sands, step out & see it all.

25.

Walking, the walkers of the sea
At a fast pace, approach, and faster,
Running, the race of the sea around us again, as the
    light falters.

26.

Deepening, the deepest water yet
Over & by the Sunken Buxey Beacon, past her,
Rushing over the waving, buoyant water.

27.

The gibber-gibber (at the eye)
Of florescent shrimps, passing
By (skipping under / against the ship)

28.

Stopped! Stretching with all the strength of our arms,
The figury, busty outboard rises to us,
Trying not to, as tricky as a mermaid, against mending.

29.

Going on to guess the lights,
The powerful draw of the power-station,
Dawning, day shows by it the modest St Peter Bradwell.

30.

Calling with the horn in my gob, mutinous at
Four mammothian tankers lined up, straight at us,
Till I see them riding to the tide, like us, anchored up.

31.

Spurting and spuming, the lovely motor
Steers us across the estuary, crossing,
Making for the marked Colne channel.

32.

So sure:
Sailing up the dark side of the mountain,
Sailing down the bright.

33.

Signing with cymbals & pipe
As we home on the hard, like pantomime,
Portending the end.

APPENDIX: A note on the Captain:

After, proud as an apple,
In the fine-sunned field of
Brightlingsea, boat-starred.

Settling the Cinque Ports

Cinques
thriving winding
greatly hoops of rhubarb

just worked iron-beans or work it
marshally shiny-handed
and they are breaking, hopeless, in order
over the powerbow, pal

but the flower, fine-yellow
foaled itself with the slope
as tin of syrup;
allow, Lydia

filly-fishing boat a'beach
of eyes up
patan patan tan
t–tapa t–tapa tapa
tanatanat tan
panapanap patan
patan tan

starving cage
ups its age

From the Seventh Sphere, like Troilus

God will never with me speak
Mercury set me in this sphere

All paper to burn and end
Like tear gas safe in sand

So gold wires are looped
Around the shiny guests

Time by little hollows made
On every side of the curve

No more hacked and toppled
In this continuum

Is crystal tree fire
Or browning timber still by line

Not like the sleep that prods the frame
Where are foggy road-shapes, background

A kid with bear-paw gloves
Puts his blood on the glass

They show me just in air
In pink forms, not just unnew

The bottom world never complete
Left made in semi-work, grounded

But these are steroids here
Giving no speed or new lot of light

Till if I crack at the tingling air
Only it is my marrow laid open.

Lacrimosation.
Cressida cannot appeal.

Here flower fields in spastic shape
Unsprayed and unscented and remade.

Similes

Like great tops
rotted to amethysts

Like singing sugar
as a scent
invisible in strength
ova wallflower, all-colour'd,
a sun-bath and signal

Or like a great wash of grease,
clinging with the tide

Like a funnel ov love
in smooth pink

As plum-glue

Like each other
slotted
in lock

Boat like tree
like hand like colour

As is anything,
partaking of –

Like the frenzied radio
ov full action, no just dream danger

unlike inconsequential ghost-ways,
nothing so personal

More like a loop of being,
a share

Like the force-blue
ov nite vision
strong-bundled fibres

Like a horizon
bringing everything into its link

Like a second sun, or this one,
seen before it's seen,
people hide in the earth from

(Like a stone stops it
or made concrete cells)

Solstice Poem

I

In the quartz prisons (radio)
or the airports
so the whining sound was a Y

The blues smudged
from the verge
to the dark blue levi's

2

The brownness of the yellow
summed for the hurt kidneys

And held models of the Earth made of brown glass
And smashed them, for sunbursts

upto
August
shaved, bored
in his brass head

3

all the
Spontaneity
Uttered from my
Near neck

4

Parts
    joined
    jokes between itselves
        as plays on

Sonnet 1

better sun
aptavit arcam – a pudding
per quam damnavit mundum
planted out his doves
fat, round like suns

Open uppart little huts of a head-house
To a lay:
Flat-chinate; showing
(Sun-hole/door)

Sonnet 2

Very whites very orange Goose
Block
White   Goose   Ocean

At Stanley (1)

Seemed absurd, unapt to talk verse on Stanley
Not for want of images
Of post-winter fields still patched white and black
Packed between house
Spaces – knew
But for living
(Words won't) want
Work in the sun.

At Stanley (2)

Is Huck,
skidding thru po-lice points like dice
with eyes and sees as a'hunting
clever sprawl-arm fighter
Gotta go –
that's my dad, said the rabbit
Pants and paws his back at back
Jesu! sez his net-man

The Sun at Foulness

stopped by the Sun at Foulness

The over-booming bronze Sun
boat along the pavement
lighted/shaded mud
with trumpets of bubbles

That we were not the only living things
in the circuit of awful flatness
back to back against
the black triangle the hull cast

Stranded in another natural element
that looked as complete
as the blue dish
to feel the silent light coming

If there was a deep bass brown
and a sky-treble or sun solo
it was all seeing it as noise
though we were parted from any sound but beak-pipes,
    and touchless.

But to be tired
and absorb the sun asleep
was real, as radiant
as the clinging phosphorous in the hull's bones.

What touches but never mates,
Gives birth but never sires,
Feeds life but never lives,
Fires but never burns away itself?

Text for Jutish or any dialect

Yes that wire loop goes back to itself and then the next
lead along goes along to the sixth pin
theres a diode there thats been broken
so what weve got to do is find out where the power leads
going to
so they come up to there and theyve been soldered on there
im fucked if i know whats wrong with it
theyre shielded so maybe theyre meant to heat up it could
just be one of the valves gone
youre getting a picture where its a reflection
it might be earth it might be earth an earth wire
i cant understand why the valves wont work unless someone
put the wrong valve in that happened with bobs telly
much warmer all the time
that box down there might be the purpose of it i reckon the
aerials useless anyway now
theyre not heating up are they if we leave it plugged in till
the smoke comes out you reckon it might work i can nick the
valves anyway
the power goes in through that box of stuff down there
    and its
mucked up
itd be worth hunting through to find out whats wrong
well the aerial comes off there doesnt it well the aerial
socket and the tuner that tunes in the stations
the thing is to find something thats burned out and causing
a short
DY87 DY87s no good
the aerial bit was heating up like a one-bar electric fire

What of you, World? What
are you, World?

I rise from the damp roads and buildings
and roll like the sun with dogs and wolves
and eagles getting their hymns
in collapsing Sion.

By the tombs
their dust cemented into ground
rot in the stones relieved and gleamed with inverted torches

Thames

River you are not man-made, but we do our best,
  unmake, remake
Rough up the skin, dress in a dirty shirt:
(So) pock-marked, hard-working, sided with docks
Niggered with coal nubs and long brown oil patches
You become likely.
                    Then we taught you spit,
To steal from ships; and give a good work shift
Sucking that mighty tide in (how many thousands of
  tons of water?)
Well pal that made us see some willingness;
Best was we taught you about bullying.

Now we are tight in bed, now tamed and dead;
O Wolfskin Wastour just you watch us winning, we'll win
                                        over you yet

Tokay

As golden-eyed
as a pure lemur
I scale the steps to the open air

On the street
on sale are windows
of glossed-black consumables: turn left

In the shop
it is hard not to gloat
it is hard not to play a tune on the bottles

Look at
the vulgar gingery carrot glint
circling the topaz-sure soul of this liquor

Thus the Romans in assuredness
laid their vines, brown-armed,
so long ago, safe to grow, in Magyar dust . . .

And the taste –
how shall I anticipate it?
The pleasing wonder of in-twinkered sun-shiver . . .

As black-bright
as a Hun-berry on the steppes
I brace my limbs to top the cork – Welcome the King!

The Train is Dismantled

baby nose to knee that fun
be a museum
the cloud and the air
flowed by throat
ascending into nose
jigsawing or filigree
titchy maze laid and
curve
the force of
a sipped river.
need of
iron food.
A red little rust for kidz' air
moving, maximises
air enjoyment
whose
the bad drum
flattened end by end
global air enjoyment 'tential.

Transactional Poems

(1) *The Influence of Prussia on the USA*

   . . . or Tugendband.
Lady of shutted eyes
A good railway network
Tin buttons
A phalanx of opal
saffron flashes, magenta hats
marching and jumping
like newsprint
and a system of mirrors
seriously tilting state to state
chucking up flags and catching
piloting is the word
and the song! a thousand-mouthéd building
with ornamental circuits above.
Two blue-steel war-socks and brass music notes
a waltz, a billion eagles
of unity and possibility
it was a necessity
steps rectangle, claims summer
alike honey and amber only.

Here is a series of clips and a captured rocket.

(2) *The Allied Influence on Japan* (*found text*)

I was one of the top men.
One evening I finished polishing my boots
I continued to excel
Father had never looked prouder
Except for Sundays the training was incessant
Methodically I performed each dive
At last it was time to sing the battle song
Plane motors – a criss-cross of sound
As if watching a film
With no recourse to justice.
Land of concrete and sun
I was going to be free
I flashed my pass for the gate
We all stood at attention
I shook and gnawed my knuckles
Filled with ideas, ideas of honour and glory
Records, documents, names of air force personnel
I donned a new uniform
Bought one of the charms
Leaving the streetcar
I banged my fist on the table, grated my chair back
Time moved like an inchworm
Hollow lockers . . . empty bed springs
Formation flying, air manoeuvres
How to make beds
The golden eagle patches on my shoulders
Laying across her tiny, child-size dresser was . . .

The Transit

The edge of the world.
a sad-enough place.
there SNOW SNOW SNOW
so go home NOW
say the police.
time/time lots
to invoke
stand back
from the bars of growth
the clutes
the plates of card
that flap at the coin-doors
along the land of the east
like ice.
unlike, like too
the flowing walls of chalk
face up,
or vault or slide
where echoes are upwritten
that are signs of sleep
(not taking) –
a vessel
a lamp
a boat
a pot
:signs, unsettled.
unguarded
after the noon.
grey is the gob
of the hatking
whose heart
is dogbig
ribs chime
in the zinc
(the sky)

before he kicks the cliffs
hymns shake loose
and slated sun-chips
there
the slant of the salmon
the twisted, white clouds
divide the sun
into multi-shafts
and wind sides it here & there
the grey mazes and glass palaces
(as something good)
speak.
On the slope
the God who is crocodile
slides at the floor of carnelian
(Stronger-than-the-mountain is his name)
you see him
turn his gaze
upon the Sun in its Sun-Barque
for then the crew halt their oars
and their dizziness has interrupted the completion of it . . .
not any other, no
recognising only what
himself put into someone else
(to give than share?
no! no! it ought to share!)
no collectors of, of
the breves of growth
in claustra
as pure cells of giant Bee
watching
that heaven with light did fill
the spaces
half footing
half vacant with
brazen scales
as hollow as

his æry plumes
tighted as
roused scales
that cap and rattle the cells of
his flaggy wing
knocking by and by as boxes
of hollow blowing
held in the air in
thick entangled knots
and on his back the
shields of red
the rimes of stems
deadly sharp

for
then the crew halted their oars
and their dizziness interrupted the completion of it

below was a roar and a running of fire
a red net in the night

Unities

a soft chime of greeting.
recognition like a football cheer.
betweenwhile he chews his paws.

a warmth of palm
on place at shoulder-blade
to make all as perfect as.

a wringing at the boot,
an unwanted grab and wake
as I snag/stumble at the wire-span.

a long tunnel of wave-radio light
in/out   creamy/black   bright/calm
way-off from sky

a great net of light
electric and levelness; and it understands me, mouthless
   on such vastness of water-show

a rough assemblage,
wrought bright growing in fingers of leaf, ruby-green
   footholds, sea-wall.

a smell safe
of sun-turning faces
at their stem to colour, burns.

a gathering of air-white
goes to show motion
bright-up   ark-down   shown on sky & ground

a lighted –
bay, day-display
a catch at no-time
pure pause of heart

The Uxbridge Workers

Invisible demolition
as near as
transparent

Ordinary jeans
a back, brick-coloured
rough, dusted fingers.

Head at work
hair turning to cement
in ridges

Or
no clothes much
but just jeans, blue thru to the sky.

Rosy-shirted
grinning
and brickpink at throat

A glazier
unsouled almost
how it bounces off his eyes.

Bright tattoos
of snakes and ladders
climbs up

One, singing at the top
unnoticed
is a crazy thrush

And lifting
broad in a block
shoulders wood-sharp

Balancing
on a vault of legs
on a curved plank

White vest
cloth-chested
glossy to paint in

Like with pulleys
topples
leaps

And a scaffolder
growing out
in new tools

Signs of ruby and blue
in the shake-wet of the head
and sun.

Two, three, more
a rainbow
mobile in line.

Arms bare.
like rods
assessing the run of the wire

A whole frame of lines
standing, stretching
on the parapet

Lifting-up
high over wavy ribs
chisel-stuff

Taut-backed, his dance of looking
as every girl comes by,
attentive like a goat

And one guy
with a trowel
nursing skulls

Over a slab-sea
lapping
at the foot of the towers
seeing the sea-bed.

Serious steel
on station,
Not gunned but guards though.

Vodka Ad

coarse sand tarot
's afront the feet
declinating slate, greensand
out the egg, way at chickling jive
walls or woman, net, boat, all the
Californian sunshine (tail-end sea)
beating sugar for the fish, or
knees

The Wild Hunt (*found text*)

Intimini sudden insect scape
vivi-patches, steep or two
red
The Sun-cottages
to move
same
brown dust
name
lanes
work hard
burning trailing snapping
foam danger-lifting fused
pale
stony snails
crisp steel-worx
fish castle
an enormous face
horses whoa! with riders hey!
dogs running behind
holes except for I'll take
winding in ridges
2p., jeans they are
ochre-wooded
deep deep like greenery, awkwardly
meadow-sweet negotiate ink-pink
fresh damp bursting great spliced things
Shakespeare
more Jane Austen & Harrison Ainsworth
carbolic sepia tulips on the 3rd day of
so-dark dogs
coming from stags
and riders silver & shaggy like
tongues attached
filling the rare grasses gutters
butter-bear

dark neck or startled
tricked by
the God a shocking livery
a little heavy

Spangle
Hinging
Table
Ruby
Coat

Mole-black
polished
solar-realeaséd
scream

In fold
scaffoldings
Seek Now to work
beserkless
rotate
been
rune
airborne
switch

breathing
streaming
an obsession
aloud
digging
grass
transfixed them
look behind
don't look
this then
looking

pattering
the others
even
look
spinning
soft
woken
burns
cotta-mist
ate
stupid
thunder
start
lid
bed
rattling
sky
angry
never
noise
alley
thrown
roan
eight
red
cows
hi
hummed
his face
alright
sorry
silly
soon
see
here are we
we are here
here are we

too hot
hill
heart
heights
of the sky
whistling
squinting
a triangle
like not
antlers
a wall
bright red
blue yellow orange
doing
skip
stop
dipping
grace
dignity
cattle
clay
bone-dry
birds
early
long
boiling flies
circle
encircles
a lot of
by
hey-hey-hey-hey yip!
hey-hey-hey-hey yip!
hey-hey-hey-hey yip!

round
toes
relax

stand
second
stop
shut
dizzy
stop
stand
second
shut
relax
tag
round
second
toes
toes
relax
shut
dizzy
stop
toes
tag

frame spun dull branches
best golden legs
look a fur of sort-blue
a deadened blue and a
deadly red
very matt / matted
hundreds and a cherry eye
all day in brightly shining skies
   they were general knowledge.

Wings

What wingz! Great targets ov blood
adhere a'shoulder, its keyboard plumes
row aside, like a power I recognise,
I slash my skin in graft, assume.

'She found a cornflower,
long-stalked & small-headed,
she picked it & stuck it thru the cardigan they'd made
    her wear.'

The old land
& the construct hedge
shows horn-colour
at the sun shine-thru

A wind ov death (glossy grey hold)
rushes thru the toy house:
every arch is uglier,
made more ridiculous.

A king reigns in the room,
purple & private and glossy-hair'd,
The angels in my hams strike up a theme
as he stands in his tent (which is the soul).

For who calles from the lupins
who stepz fron the wallflowers
but rank-haired lunacy,
his local ambush.

All in the crystals ov snow
the plantless queen
holds south
with her player-whales

Between every wave is thunder.
What a chasm
– die Millionen! –
the Sun rises from.

Every sparkling living cell
tuned to salute another;
burialz and minerals too
chance the air.

Zoo Keeper

tempestu-
ous a ocean-token
to dolly air 'at's a'
waste-with-magic or
whirled curls/pearls
face it all bright, grim

issuing with growling
az a mist like a magenta
soundful & holy & blank, bole and apple – clerestory
closer: sweet-angle a' then circumflex then silvered – this
    shovelling
will be bulging head of Spring, swift she will

Reynard got fur togs in his job
and me Ysengrim
chases an aeroplane
& tailing the sun (vauxio custar')
az I won on, tiny like tagman

there's scarce grail-flower
not in the pots, not in the tins –
not in the windows, walk, bins – a bagatelle
till the roof's groaning
and plausible w/ the
words of a god
shaking and tramping, eager t'its guillotine, I ll keep you

Brian Catling

WRITTEN ROOMS AND PENCILLED CRIMES

(A Sinistral Cloister of Prose, Trespassed by Voices from Earlier Books)

For Len and Lily: My parents, my friends

Contents

Introduction

Brian Catling's work explores the texture of the boundaries of his imagination. The ideas produced from this imagination can find their manifestation in a performance, a sculptural installation or a written text. Each of these three discrete areas possesses its own pulse and rhythm, yet they are organically bound together, by structure, images and obsession.

Written Rooms and Pencilled Crimes began in a filmic role, as an attempt to capture the elusive qualities of the performances and installations, both transient experiences lost in time. The texts quickly took on their own momentum, drawing from the other two areas of activity and consequently feeding images and ideas back into both, re-forming the performances, as they in turn unlocked a new possibility for an installation, which subsequently produced a new text.

The title *'Written Rooms and Pencilled Crimes'* provides a key to all three areas, and to this inter-relationship. *'Written'* suggests the physical reality and marking process of Catling's installations; whilst *'Pencilled'* evokes the transient, quickly 'erased' nature of his performances. *'Rooms'* are conjured in his installations, through a sensing of, and attuning to, the physical and psychic qualities of the particular space in which each is made. *'Rooms'* are also the environments within which his performances occur, and spaces described by the texts.

'Crimes' are interpreted here as actions against the continuum of normal human activity, as performed by the dispossessed. The melancholic archetype of the dispossessed and its activity as a metaphor for the human search for knowledge and meaning are central tenets of Catling's work. This search is articulated

in the performances by the 'operator', and in the installations, presented as vast mythical landscapes, in the form of a path, mapping a journey. The texts describe both the room and the crime, the archetype stealing through the folds of words. They are sometimes violent, expressing the extreme point of energy at which some kind of transformation takes place. The 'operator's' role recalls the story of Frankenstein or his mythic Jewish eastern precursor the Golem, in which the dispossessed persona is given unhuman power but whose understanding is less than human, and so becomes impossible to control.

Such a persona also echoes the concept of the divine idiot in Sufi parables, whose clumsy actions conceal the essence of knowledge. In Catling's work this low-life creature also represents an angelic presence (the Golem's opposite) which, having fallen to earth from Hypothenia, tries to articulate itself into being. This other 'self', which Catling becomes during his performances and which moves stealthily through his texts, comes into existence through a process of transformation. The almost unsayable act of passing through oneself into one's non-self is at the centre of gnostic thought. Along with the insistent theme of repeated failure it is at the heart of all Catling's work, as it is of Beckett's.

This transformation distinguishes Catling's work from allegory. His performance is not acting but direct experience, and in his installations and text the properties of particular substances, objects or words are placed together in order to break the surface and expose what is beneath.

In so doing, a fine balance is retained between the absurd and the sinister, the exposed and revealed, the ethereal and the material, and between the domestic and the spiritual. In the performances and installations the latter could be an act, such as the washing of hands, or an object or substance, such as a carpet, or bread. The texts express the same balance through words, the places and objects they describe and the implication of the book as a mystical and domestic object. Similarly, opposing features from the installations, such as the severity of extreme temperatures, are also written.

Words shape the texts as materials, gestures and movements direct a performance, displacing the apparent. The clashing of materials and hint of violence this involves can be traced back to Catling's earlier poems, where all the concerns of the later work are held within a crystallised structure. '*Written Rooms and Pencilled Crimes*' release these concerns into the air. They are like performances seen from a distance, windows onto the other areas, articulated inside their own unity.

Chrissie Iles, October 1989

WRITTEN ROOMS AND
PENCILLED CRIMES

i

In a square room with no windows a glass tube runs along the walls, close to the ceiling: it is joined at both ends making a continual square. It is filled with water. In the water swims an eel. The eel is not much smaller than the tube; it cannot turn around and must swim in one direction. The water is kept fresh and aerated by an automatic unit set in the wall; this device also injects food at regular daily intervals.

Running along the bottom of the wall on the floor is a trough. It also makes a continual square. (A visitor to the room must step over it on entering.) The trough contains crystals of sodium suspended in oil.

In the centre of the room are five cast lead models of eels.

Should the obvious cruelty and futility of the room overcome its beauty, the means are there to destroy it and to free its captive.

Water and sodium have the most violent chemical reaction when mixed.

ii

An angel waits in an hermetic chamber. It kneels in respect and seems to be communicating with its hands; a kind of concerned agile violence equally akin to the reaching of the blind and the tactile spatial understanding of the more esoteric martial arts. The angel is made of asbestos. The method of construction is crude: it is bolted through splintered holes; it is strapped with opaque tapes; it is tied with soft core iron wire. Only the hands show a degree of obsession and care in execution.

The chamber seems to be out of focus. (It is viewed from the outside through a tight porthole.) There is a tinge of blue in the air. The door is heavy, made of thick steel. If the door is opened the viewer is confronted by a blast of air. A vast concealed fan blows a gale in the limited space of the room. The air is filled with finely ground particles of blue asbestos. This powder can hardly be seen; it will only be perceived later in the pain of the most curious spectators.

iii

Nine men stand in a circle. They wear breeches of fine black cloth; they are bare-chested. They have pointed Vandyke beards and wear high white ruffs about their throats. In the shadows at the back of the same room sits a woman. She is indistinct in the gloom, but appears to be holding something close to her.

From a leather bucket, water is taken in cupped hands by one of the men who passes it to his neighbour, who in turn passes it around until it reaches the bucket again. Inevitably, water is spilt at each transaction, causing a broken circle to be drawn on the floor, and less water to be returned. As the procedure continues the men move back to increase the size of the circle.

A low discordant whistle is heard; it is that sound a human would make in an attempt to mimic the wind. As the water is passed, each man joins in this imitation. As the circle is increased, the sound becomes louder. By the time the water is spent the circle and the sound are both large and fragmented. The men with dripping hands leave the room.

The woman moves, slowly in silence she walks forward. She stoops carefully and turns the bucket over. She sits on it. She is wearing a simple white dress of tissue paper. She exudes that beatific but absent resonance often seen in early images of the madonna. This impression is amplified by the maternal way she cradles the object in her arms. It is child size. It is a misshapen cylinder of ice. A fine wire or tube protrudes from its sealed interior. Occasionally she moves her burden from one arm to the other. It is melting quickly; the water and the friction of action erode and tear her flimsy dress. As the object decays a sound is heard, faint and tinny. It is the sound of that same spoken artificial wind played through a small, cheap loudspeaker inside the ice.

The object is now completely gone; only splinters and water remain in a pool at her feet. Most of the lower half of her dress lies in wet tatters, a few twisted strands cling to her legs. She is naked except for a small part of the upper bodice; from there the wire hangs down between her legs. The small loudspeaker hovers above the pool, moving slightly with the action of her breathing.

She stands, picks up the bucket and leaves the room.

iv

Sweet Ishmali kept to her room; in fact, she was imprisoned there. Her adultery was being paid off with suffocation, kept inexorably at bay by her ingenuity. When her four-star cage was finally opened, belief was confounded by a treasury of unknown objects and attachments, constructed from the broken and reassembled furnishings of the room. The nature and mechanics of the things she had cannibalized could never have been clearly known to her. Her tribal childhood among the arid buzz of the seasonal villages could never have prepared her for the interior of the massive colour television that once dominated the centre of this plush, air-conditioned hotel room: now turned inside out. A rich brutal ingenuity had transformed it into a series of wired-together props or harnesses that littered the wrecked space. In these allusive aids could also be found remnants of a bath tub, toilet cistern, carpet, picture frames, shredded light fittings. A myriad of discrete objects splintered from their function. Her bed was the concentrated centre of the event. The devices here were attached to a series of crude bells that had been constructed from glasses, cups, a cathode ray tube, spoons and an unused toothbrush. It is supposed these were effective alarms that saved her from fatal movements in her sleep. The fear of her dreams is only to be imagined.

Other women of her tribe would have given themselves up to their inevitable fate, but Ishmali was proud. She had married well to a rich young chief who had been educated abroad and was now climbing the fire ladder into politics. Her neck grew in value as their marriage lengthened. The first rings were made of base alloys and dense iron, she had grown with these from childhood to pubescence; then at marriage they had been exchanged for gold, a new one added each year.

She held her distended and oddly inflexible head high in the rich and powerful circles in which they now moved.

After the sentence had been pronounced and the rings re-moved, she must have literally carried her head, for normally the unsupported neck would fold and suffocate, or its thin brittle vertebrae would snap and announce the end. But she would not let go of her rigid but precipitous hold on life. The strangeness of the devices was partially due to the fact that they must have been made with one hand at a tense angle, while the other extended the head across the floor, or bed or chair, or perhaps held it aloft like some morbid fruit displayed in a practised and horrifying act of juggling.

When her sad body was carried from the boudoir, it was not because of her lack of concentration or skill, but ironically due to the fatigue of the materials she had used. A splinter from a five-foot prop made from a hat stand, a standard lamp and an ashtray had pierced the soft space beneath her left ear. Death must have been painful and complex.

The hotel management, who had only ever left food and fresh linen outside the room, were perplexed by the situation and the irrational objects that fluttered in it. After some debate they condemned the contents to surreptitious incineration. It was lately rumoured that some of the things found their way into a German museum of contemporary art. It must be supposed that the curator found suitable aesthetic potency in their merciless invention.

V

Along that vast bleak eastern coast, high in a turret room of an old hotel grown weary of occupation, two strangers make love. The moon rises across the luminous rhythm of their bodies. The sea is held in a circular pulse that is beyond scale of eye or window. Spine becomes a seeing bow, using breath for its taut string.

Here, flesh can be exchanged for light, heat or motion.

The city sinew can only be named time, and washed to distance by the hush of tide.

vi

The hermit's task is to absorb the demons of his chosen desert, to funnel their appetites and magnitude through his open observing soul. The central station of the city is the wilderness for this urban anchorite. His locusts and honey are stored in metal wastebins or scuffed under rank public seats. It is necessary to erase all self image, the ferreting for edible scraps efficiently rubs the surface away. Newspapers bind him against the cold and the night winds. Sleep is found cleated in architectural contrivance or in the disused caves of plywood hoarding.

His isolation is a numerical thing, calculated in faces and lives. He must see every face in every day, notching each, consuming their portraits from the eddying rush-hour swarm.

To tear the flesh he must also collect farewells and greetings. The emotional poles of each must be balanced in number and expression or his spirit will be taken. His strength and resolve are sanctified by the angels who clatter their gills to sign and speak the names of future edens.

vii

The ceiling is too low; it is only five feet from the floor, which is of pale wood. The room is very white and its brilliance is cherished by a group of polished black marble boxes that crouch on the floor.

Things seemed more normal outside in the reception area. There were Italian steel chairs and a desk with a typewriter. The walls were covered with expensively framed miniatures. These works, in contrast to their display, seem crude; they are not complete pictures but fragments, details torn or cut from some larger area. They are essentially primitive; designs of flowers, birds and snakes; the occasional name interlaced with a heart or some other sentimental device. Even the materials seem to be basic; the inks have faded or in some cases lost their focus; the surface is shrivelled, porous, and covered in fine dead hair. Attention is drawn from them by an illuminated sign above the door of the low room which bids us 'enter'.

It is difficult to stay still in this stunted room; the stooped position a viewer would have to take is more comfortable when accompanied by a slight forward motion.

A faint rubbing noise is heard from the centre of the room; on examination one of the boxes has a glass side. A pair of hands are moving carefully in its confined space. It must be assumed that the rest of this occupant is in the room below or under the floor. The glass is thick and distorted at the edges, so the wrists cannot be seen. The hands touch each other, the glass and the inner surfaces of the marble. The searching and caressing appear to be both sensitive and strong like the hands of a lover, skilful, quiet and keen; an urgency of restraint. The hands might be oblivious of the viewer or they might stop and point or attempt to hide in the unfocused spaces of the box.

The sign above the door demands that we 'leave'.

Outside, it is noticed that the typewriter keys are meshed and tangled together.

viii

Returning to the old nursery was not totally unpleasant; it was the circumstances of the move that were so distasteful. The influenza that held him captive for two weeks had turned into a violent lung infection, uncontrollable spasms of coughing kept him awake most of the night. What was worse, they kept his wife awake as well. She was a woman of lopsided emotions, her own spindle of existence being distorted by unknown past events. In a cowardly attempt to offer confidence to her on a servile plate, he had long since encouraged her to nurture the key to his own emotional imprisonment. Her bouts of sub-polar rage and silence had forged the key to a high-tensile weapon.

When the coughing developed a chorus of wheezing between the outbursts, the lock was rattled. He could no longer occupy his tidy pine bed on the east side of their marital dormitory. The acoustics made his irritating sibilations malicious to her; a noise designed and projected to keep her awake.

His bed was stripped and carried to the old nursery. His new lodging.

The odd word, or something like it, caught his attention at moments when he drifted in a medicated nimbus in the softening colour of the musty room. The coughing had gone. The wheezing was long and pointed at both ends, a tendril that fluctuated whispers and piped voices into a converging eerie syntax. He started to listen carefully to the intonation of this foreign untongued oration. He could hear punctuation and expression being articulated in the fluid whistles. He instinctively knew this ethereal sing-song was waiting to tell him of the dreams he had never had. And it did; his cot was becoming a confessional of oracular vision. When his hearing and his need were tuned – and his head tucked closer to his chest – the benevolent genji in his lungs would whisper soliloquies of memory that carried back across the apologetic rubble of his compromised life; back over a landscape ill-lit by misplaced hope and congealed passion; back and through a shimmering awareness of growing power. This was becoming alarmingly balanced by a quietening of the voice of his guide; there was a healing to its mouth of volume.

He ceased the medication, reduced the heating in the tiny room and opened the window enough to let the cold air unseal the flow of dream.

Rolled in a ball, ear to chest, a blanket over him to screen off the unnecessary outside noise; he listened again. Like this, contracted tight, he was carried further on the journey back, or it may have been forward. In the timeless light that spun from the incantation, it was impossible to say; his body became an accelerated circular track, humming to silence in the quiet room.

ix

In Trondheim, in the high north, is a vast tank of still water. The town sipped with irritation during the months it took to fill. It is matt black to discourage light-active spores and simple plants from inhabiting its polished measured interior.

Its volume is such that the curvature of the earth can be seen and calibrated across its surface. Wave action can be simulated. Small, highly coloured boats are sensored and drawn across its mass to test the design of their symmetrical perfection.

Spidered rigs are leant against its artificial sway. These are its spoken purposes; there is another, unsaid. When the toys are shelved and the computed illustration of function is unplugged and the lights switched off, it becomes a tear, salting in its manmade duct, pulsing in sympathy to the dying oceans and seas.

x

Another deserted room, its history functional, economic, and unquestionably material. Its details undisturbed: peeled paint, chipped plaster, uneven constant usage: a room where people have worked, aged and dented all the angles of respect and time.

The floor is scattered with remnants of previous occupation; paper, disconnected telephones, wires, unknown scraps of wood and metal, cups, dust and any other thing without individual numinosity. A sheet of frosted glass of irregular size is set into the floor where it is smeared with dust to blend it into its surroundings.

Hundreds of needles are strewn across the surface of the glass. Each needle is tipped in a solution of cobra venom and a suspension gum.

The needles will move in a circular motion, each pointing forward. The motion will be uncertain, slow and sometimes nervous. This movement in the room will first be seen peripherally, then it is hoped studied at some detail. Should curiosity cause interference there is a high possibility of the event being lethal.

A circular electro-magnetic disc rotates beneath the surface of the glass, the underside of the glass is finely painted with dashes and spots of a non-magnetic paint.

The plate is attached to a silent electric motor, which in turn is connected to a control box; this box also controls the magnetic field of the disc.

An interrupted supply of electricity to the movement and the field gives the needles their jerky, uncertain, movement. It is important the movement is not mechanical, but rather the motion of shoals of fish or the directed twitching causation often seen in the paranormal.

from VORTICEGARDEN

Moon surgeon

Moon surgeon
dazzles in transparent air,
entwining the
cosmic dragon
onto the rubber hand.

And travellers stumble into
night's artillery
crazed in subterranean swamp-
fever.
Mineral clock unwinds a sprung
water tongue.

A ghost is being built from the more
solid things.

To journey longer and blister

To journey longer and blister
around the vegetable eruption,
its thermal violence-
eating tantrum.

Or mid-europe among smoke & trees.
Treatment varies painfully
but squeezes out mephitic pleasures
under weighted pinball moons.

But being earthed & unmasked
adrift on the pesthouse clinker;
to journey is a cancerous deceit
for the monkish leather android.

He tried the gas cylinder walk

He tried the gas cylinder walk
that lead him into the fur-nailed
history.
In coma
the instrumentation of legend
ticked & flickered
wildly.

Crawling from a
species mash.
Bearing withdrawal symptoms
across the vegetable lip.

Alive in the drizzle wet dream
with blood.

With his hand he broke
the neck of the wind.

It's not in

It's not in
drowning
when the files are locked
for future police.
Things swell in boxes
growing swelter black.

Others dry to a husk
pores and stitching
ink in detail
hard/fine/stipple.

There is a hunt
in this moon chrome year.
It ripens
the woman-stained coat.
Chicken slashed petrol milk
smells above cooking.

It gives the mind
a chinese burn.

The arteries from the house wind out

The arteries from the house wind out
curling their sinews of incident; coil
the loophole in identity. A dream of
yesterday's polaroid dialogue:
sulking wet colour, the remnant burnt
then chilled for safety.

Through the gap the dark can drain
sucking light motors in, their
magnetic weight screening the trivial
domestic triggers.

The house frozen
preserved in light
pinnacled by star metal.
Stairs and rooms evilly constructed
in tone, & age.

The shadows are German here
but the light is older.

When the bone-one steps through the skin

When the bone-one steps through the skin:
its embrace quickens the cold.
At the apex of the street, the grip well known,
a drowning embrace
a saved friend.
From the cold we spin into the freezing rot.
Grosz sees it & calls it the end.

The window head buzzes in warmth.
From the black rigid street a blackening face appears.
The growing cold tightens & angles the lines.
Soundlessly the bone-man steps out of the dying one
viciously gripping him
a white ice saviour.

The old fog we carry

The old fog we carry
disapproves of its host, finding the
bound book dated.

Outer drama smogs the epic.

Grandville sees death in smock & rucksack,
visiting the watchmakers; a stool has turned,
a hand grasp freezing, the chimpanzee shade-tilted
face gapes into the glass on the skeletal hook.
Fifteen minutes to eleven on a busy day.

A scratch has already appeared on the chrome surface.
Teethlike the mist sharpens, displaying fear veneered
with politeness.
What I have carried has been a vampire to its
movements, resenting the book that it finds
dated.

Working on hearsay

Working on hearsay
decaying whispers
smears;
well lit films
rusted into 3
channeled
veneered abattoir.

Odd red moons
bend the savage
daydream
& ease
the telephone
blemish that aches
into the second day.

From the shifting
link
performing weaker
verbal surgery
& failing to revive
the reflection of
this hybrid vector.

Moment bones

Moment bones
smother
after the act,
indoors registering
cunning

Outdoors
flown to register
magic: not knowing
of the crazed screaming
canopy,
birds
under total eclipse.

The metal needs
a flesh cushion
before the act
to record
& forget
a fever of cogs.
The gumming with guano
matting the sequence
motor.

From the quiet bell

From the quiet bell
an arctic sound: ice in forming
bends a beat on the tissue of hearing.
Retreating heat rinses the skin edge,
red under white
outside a canopy of wind.

The mess of roads congeal
the fainter track ticks with interior
ice.
Thinking across library bands, but close in.
Leaning from mortise knowledge that would bleed us.
Seeking only that wrought from the maps
of nomadic reason.

From behind, hearing spins the head compass
being strafed / snow
lowered in the well on the frozen
log raft.
The cairn of books marking me.

From vast

From vast
loomings
hung on the eyes
of hinges, shadows
behind arthritic
shields.

The recess of home
notched
into the spiral track
of the loadstone motor.
The image frame locked
hissing in the coned
momentum.

from DAS KRANKE TIER

The horns they rise

The horns they rise
from the centre
the broken space cleared
in trophy for the
eye

splintered barrel
wobbles out jellied
projections, melted
off from inferior
sulphur stuffing.

Set to clash
cordite hair
in nucleic comedy.
Rust in apathy
sets the pace.

In the space of healing

In the space of healing
all failure is automatically sewn closed,
sealed
the triangular cavity where the blind enzymes
step in clatter, their detailed sound
cutting up through the lecture hall.

Pass by
the loosely knotted seepage
is without word,
it's only squash or early born
tossed in rush/hour.

The space is erotic
hemmed in by oxygen.

It bares in

It bares in

on powerfully noted acts
a semblance of learning
(clustering)
                some jaundice bonemeal edge
                half rotted in anaemic doubt.
Later when a somnambulist
wind heaves through the house.
                A paring of dreams, blown
                about the night's trapped
                reflections gleaming in
                street sodium.
From these battered
externalised flights
a picture is tightened
                another revenging poverty,
                teething.

Testimony

Testimony
is piped out in thick rubber tubes.
Tighter relations escape
from thread bare valves,
a child paste
blubber between
the families.

There is the non-surgical
older in its stars.
With the discolouration of cinema age
pleated about its aim
but that waits, the sticky
enclosure of the cell resisting
all pressure with mute sexuality.

from **VOX HUMANA**

Suspicion

Suspicion
is the carrier
of staves, hand set
at brush fire, hedge poison
control,
          But it is a french town
          that quivers in the approach.
          Resistance
          drooping in the heavy wind
          & hope
          of reburnished and transmuted
          cruelty.
The wands
are cut from the very path
by new and expectant hands,
          but the moon
          has swung somatic change along
          the settled streets.
The gift
is razored by thorns & the language wrapper
soon falls away
sweated by vinegar.

Hormone clackers and cheap light

Hormone clackers and cheap light
announce the arrival
& punk sunbeams don't reach the waste bin
and collide against the decaying arc
of dog-end neutrons, only to fall bitterly
without even that recollection.

Hand works aimlessly
trying to find the power
to convert
donjon gas to cathedral voice/elaboration
defying musk.

The office of the dead is filled with heating
machines, monitors that gauge and adjust.
Broken faces that have felt the distance of prayer,
falling through to skulk beneath pelvic desk.

Clerical security incubi
occupies the ink driving seat.
From that cuticle nib divided
spits the flame

the breath of its hunger curdling bloodfood
outside the intimate lead of stained glass.

The square of commerce

The square of commerce
where they were torn & burnt,
boiled over oxtail manuscripts
thick and overt with sinister
mobility
            cooking becomes a healing process
            for sacrificed meat; fats & water
sperm the crowd.
It's not play in its month
big finance cuts severing
the rim of architecture,
the scene is punched into close-up,
boils and scabs are cheaper.
            But this is
            a retail performance
            unstapled from guide books.

            Brass plate cleated
            over saint dripping

            polished
            between
            county & diocese.

It issues from the box

It issues from the box;
furniture of books
the landscape with opaque trees
is half the composition,
avian diagram posing an eye,
now a delta
now a hook. You may expect angels here
without wool & sugar.

More of oak
or ash
with dreadful insect potential.

Take it to the other window
swollen with sun,
itch the gris gris loose
to freeze the splintered tears of that
timber mother.
Except the nail driven in prayer
it cusps the root
of possible wing.

WRITTEN ROOMS AND
PENCILLED CRIMES

---

xi

There are five cast-iron fireplaces in the medium-sized room. Five maids dressed in starched uniforms of black and white scurry through the room's oppressive and dusty heat, each attending their own fire.

With curtseying invisibility, they sweat and flutter while carrying coals; they mutter and flick strands of wet hair from their foreheads, while poking the heaped coals or sweeping the dunes of ash into copper buckets.

There is nothing else in the room; its windows are sealed shut, heavy curtains dropping from the ceiling. There are two small corridors from the room. One is piled and blocked with gleaming coal; tons of it. The other is almost filled with a mound of ash. This simple balance cannot be adjusted from the outside. Supplies of material and elemental sustenance offer only the crudest of calibrations.

xii

They seem of the lowest order, perhaps recruited temporarily from the streets. They sit in brown warehouse coats chain-smoking cheap, stale cigarettes. They talk, these three, in intimate guffaws. The conversation seems vulgar in its gesture.

Before them sits a large brown paper parcel, over them is suspended a dim light bulb. They seem unaware of the heavily bandaged apparition that sits a few metres from them; a shrouded figure that sways slightly in its difficult shunted breathing. A soft melodic whine is heard from this living mummy. It is noted that its legs, or what should be legs, are bandaged together to form a tubular tail, fin-shaped where the feet should be. One is reminded of the basic image of a mermaid or man; this impression is tuned by a suggested smell of fish, but this could be subjective. A man in a white coat joins this disjointed company; he sits at a portable table, puts on earphones and stabs at a typewriter. After some time he stops, looks up and calls to the bandaged one in some unknown harsh language. It is a commanding tone but there is no response; he snaps his fingers at the trio of workers, they sluggishly – and with no apparent interest – start to unwrap the parcel. Three or four layers are removed, the bandaged one jolts into consciousness. As if stung or punched into speech, it begins to sing in an eerie voice that is high and wavering. The white-coated man presses his earphones close to his head, listens carefully then begins to write again. After three or four minutes, the voice stops. The writer becomes agitated and shouts again, his face becoming white with anger. No response. He then shouts at the workers who have just lit another cigarette; they unwrap more layers of paper in the same indifferent manner. A fine sprinkling of red powder is covering their area of action and their hands. They start to smoke more avidly. The connection between this parcel and the mind of the interrogated is unknown, but the voice begins to call again in a fiercer, more painful manner. The typist begins again, until the sound fades. The writer is even more furious this time.

He pounds the table, spitting draconian commands at the

workers. They pull the package apart; dust, smoke and paper scatter around. Above, the light bulb flickers and increases in magnitude. The bandaged one rocks back and forth, singing in a higher, faster way; the typewriter clatters; the entire ensemble are enraptured in a moment of activity.

The parcel is gone. Just paper and string, dust and stamped-out cigarettes. The singer clutches its head in its hands and bends forward. The writer listens carefully, then packs up his equipment and leaves. Water starts to drip from the bandaged head, making splashes around the imagined tail.

The workers light up again and shuffle away, mumbling in a distracted way.

Water now pours from the head; the figure is static and shrunken. The torrent floods the floor, running into the red dust and paper where it makes a soaked and collapsed puddle.

xiii

There is a flat, consisting of three rooms, in a quiet part of a distant country town. It is the set for the death of two doomed lovers. Nothing moves in an obvious manner. But it all shudders every ninety seconds, it is an inward movement; the surface texture of reality agrees to stay constant. It is the molecular flesh and bones of normal things; the oven, the bed, the record player, the framed prints that shiver and realign themselves in a continuum of control. It might be pity that moves here, but it could equally be fear or disgust.

The death itself was not a bodily thing. They numbed their spirits with a sullen toxic mixture of common sense and guilt. They used the vicious torpic edge of separation to slit the heat from their blood. They committed this act so they could leave and keep their physical existence intact.

The only noticeable thing about the rooms is their absolute stillness.

xiv

The wilful concentration of the child, fixed at the hub of his reality, was enormous. It spun without notice on the linoleum floor, a centrifuge made invisible by its agreement with time. A thing not to be interrupted or touched. It made a gap for the mother to step out of her leashed day. She dreamed and listed, future plans opened out, years making themselves available to her like rungs; so that she might climb out into their influence, savouring the warmth on her ageing skin.

The child sat in a heap of small plastic animals; farmyard creatures, jungle beasts, mythic monsters, dinosaurs and domestic pets. The scale of the menagerie varied, giving an unpredictable and alarming irregularity; a chicken could overshadow a bear. This was of no consequence to the child, who vitalised and enclosed them in his own taxonomy of need. In his play there was something furtive; he would look around to gauge that the attention of his mother was elsewhere. Occasionally she would jolt from her reveries to his gaze and not understand the expression she found there. The moment would eventually become dislodged by a nervous smile or a word or by one of the links in the dry electric chain of radio voices that played between them, being rattled. The endless equator of masculine abstract violence drearily tightening the world only served to delineate their day; a clock of drones.

The animals were changing, their physical syntax being sliced and skinned. A blade had been stolen from his father's armoury of tools, the kitchen hob had been used when unguarded. Glue and saws had knotted the morphogenesis of this bestiary. The child was surgically cataloguing a new ark of the malformed; species and fusions of knubbled plastic that became feasible and grotesque. Hybrids of a secret need to see what would happen if.

XV

The bar was full; a Saturday night when this essentially masculine place was bejewelled by the mournful women of the weekday drinkers. This night was their given opportunity to grace a bar stool in their spouses' time-worn drinking corner. It is the proletarian sector of the city, all the pubs are stiff with overdressed dreams of wealth and power. Gold talismans of violence are worn to reflect the glare and the noise in these bullpens of pride and limitation.

Strangers are not known here. There is a brutal territoriality to each bar that gleams beneath the laughter and smoke. The outsider is not noticed at first, his presence is so minimal, he stands pressed to the centre of the bar, sipping a small beer. He skilfully allows the odour of his existence and alienation to bleed out. He wires his salient antenna to the opposite pole of those around him. He slowly becomes a beacon of nervous, introverted trepidation. He employs spilling, shuffling, staring and mumbling to amplify his wince, so that his noisy status of victim is seen by all, indeed some of the inhabitants might be ready to act on it, so aggressive is the paradox of its impunity.

This is when the chorus arrives. One by one they enter and place themselves around the room. They are men of minotaur lineage, fist keepers of street gnosis. Broken faces, bodies grown in a stance of muscular threat. They are identically suited. They enter the throng at thirty-second intervals, until the walls of the bar are dark with their presence.

They speak to nobody. Twenty of this shoal now stand along the perimeter of the room, formal and aloof, their hunting eyes making spokes to the hunched shoulders and back of the twitching intruder who refuses to acknowledge their invasion.

He begins to move, a strange, shrugging spasm; in it his posture changes, a formal confidence dusting the grimy fear from his twitching skin.

He stands erect and implacable. Quietly, but with slow determination, he takes things from his pockets and places them on a cleared area on the wet bar; a squat night candle, a box of matches, a square of white silk.

The candle is carefully lit; his hand protecting the flame from any gusts that will not occur in the captivated room. The candle is gently placed on the silk, the matches returned to his pocket.

He turns and leaves the bar, the suited mob leave after him in a quick indifferent exit.

The night light flickers when the door closes, the customers turn to it, and themselves, for some kind of answer.

Outside the team move on to the next bar.

Myth can be broken and reformed by forcing comparisons.

xvi

It could once have been a dog. Now it is difficult to say. Half
its body has been removed and replaced by a complex harness of
plastic and aluminium, electrical panels infest its surface. From
the rear of this hybrid extends one long articulated rod, the
first joint of which works like a rudimentary leg or stilt for
the creature. The rod extends from there to the mid-point of
the room where it fuses with a large neon cage. This structure is
an articulated cube of light, a frame just smaller than the room.
There is a universal joint at each of its eight intersections; the
joint is powered by hydraulic pistons that cling to its outer
casing. The cube is the only source of illumination in the room.
It is capable of extreme distortion which seems reliant on the
impulse and activity of the creature. The room is thick with the
smell of excrement and electricity. The wounded thing moves
with a sickening yet hypnotic hopping crawl, attempting to
find food among the decayed mass of plates that litter the floor.
The cube becomes activated by its search, twisting its magical
perspective and casting smooth echoed shadows around the
room. Nameless cans of animal food and an opener sit on
a low shelf at a convenient angle to the door; this gives the
viewer the opportunity of leaving, without the damaged beast
making a bolt for freedom and perhaps causing strange and
hostile abstract configurations of the cube.

xvii

In a pedestrian underpass in a derelict part of the city is a curved wall; it winds through graffitied half-light that is abrased by the roar of traffic and the breath of diesel fumes. Sunlight sits above; it is connected to the wall by stairways at either end. This is a place to pass through quickly, an abused urban map of necessity. A cry is heard, a continual guttural human shout; it is that insane, drunken ramble that is coughed out, a tongue of the lost, common in all languages.

He is seen creeping along the wall, pressing himself against the stained and chipped tiles. His arms are out-stretched, fingers inching him along. He is crouching or kneeling, one leg trailing in the puddles of urine and rain water.

We move faster to avoid contact with this uncertain man. The noise changes in its passage, the broken edges clear and sharpen. The clotted phlegm volume opens out. At our mutual mid-point it is another voice; soft, high and clear. It is now an angelic troubadour sound, locked in a velocity of prayer or love.

We pass, trying to avoid the eyes. As we depart the voice begins to crack, beyond the dim centre. It fractures back into that shamble of madness we heard before. By the time we both reach light it is folded into the indifferent choir of traffic.

xviii

They have been sent keys; the office workers who strut this territory with the certainty of possession. Some have been followed or watched, their conversations overheard. Some have been selected at random.

The keys and the addresses arrive at their doors without comment or direction. Some are thrown away in irritation, some are lost by indifference, some are turned by curiosity.

The large, top-floor office they enter is empty; the bewildered client stands key in hand, pointing it like an invitation to explain his trespass, or a torch to illuminate his purpose. The windows are sealed by opaque screens, dim and spacious. There is one bright spot, a bar of sunlight falls across a single, trunk-sized stone near the centre of the room. It is dark and featureless but smooth and regular in its form, a giant pebble. The floor near the stone has been washed and it offers a bruised gleam to the balanced gravity of the mass. A slit in the ceiling lets the massive unfolding of the skies sit tightly on the surface below. The abnormality is only seen after hours of meditation. The bar of light is in constant embrace with the stone, it never wanders with the moving day across the room. The technically minded will imagine the possible machine on the roof, the complexity of its timing, its lenses and mirrors catching and turning the sun to standstill. Those who become deeply enmeshed in its glamour will see that it prolongs twilight, pinning dusk on the rock an hour after darkness.

It must be a temple clock, a shrined motor to contemplation, casting a prayer on the solid altar of matter.

Only the technically minded will know that the stone is in fact skilfully polished and coloured polystyrene.

xix

When God gave the first humans consciousness, he whispered advice under his celestial breath as they shivered their way out of Eden: 'obscure thyselves'. Every tribe or half-simian with the ingenuity has since learnt to brew or distil fluids and vapours to occasionally relieve themselves of the intolerable jabber of thought; to numb their magnificent senses just enough to sensually smudge judgement and nerve.

A good bar is a sanctum to this need. *Au Metro* was a cathedral. The shabby cave is gone, disappeared between rare pilgrimages. Now gutted, degraded into a fourth-hand furniture shop; peeling *Ricard* labels and disconnected light fittings marking the old perimeter of noise; the dance music of the Sunday flea market in Liège.

The city has dignity on the rim of its poverty, using bankruptcy like spit to polish the once-expensive tone of its grand boulevards. This was the armaments centre of Europe for hundreds of years. The cordite now draining to the east leaving the shell of industry empty.

The dance and the market continue. Objects and voices pawing each other, swelling the smells of human meeting. To some extent the trade is incidental, a vast nomadic museum of history and food curating the odd to its centre.

There is always a gritty pearl compressed by such life, a transmutation hutch where fiction grows in direct proportion to the dwindling of fact. *Au Metro* was such a gem. There it was impossible to imagine a fiction larger than the incident occurring at the next table.

Alice and the Red Queen could *petit déjeuner* here, their prime ugliness and alienation would be relished. Their quest for the impossible expanded.

The first dance begins at eight-thirty, by ten the over-enthusiastic, and the horizontal, jabbering harmonica player, are being gently shovelled outside.

It's not big enough for a stage or a pit, but it does have a shelf. The hunched musicians are folded with their instruments, hard under the ceiling. From there the crabbed sway and pulse will animate the demi-mondaine; the children, old men and police who cannot resist the charm of its puppetry.

The exhausted tables of drinkers are politely served by the resident staff; the six-foot transsexual beams down, her stubble splintering the pancake, her milk-blind eye smiling into the next glass of pastis. Her companion is even older, an ink wash of a lounge toad starched with Dracularian elegance; the ancient white hair dubbed into negative, a blue-black trickle pinned under the arm of his heavily tinted spectacles. These are the heralds of a cast list that would read as fiction; their ornate humanity guides, serves and protects their patrons with wisdom and humour.

Au Metro is sadly missed, miraculous things were made there. The echo of the amplification is kept, a stain of the split lives that outside would be violently mopped up, cleaned away. Obscurity is to be toasted, to be praised in advance of the obsessive uniformity that wields the broom against the beauty of abnormal growth.

The pearl must not be polished but wondered at, paring it down to a sanitary brightness will lose the depth of its precious reflection. We can only conserve the nutrient beds of night soil and decay in the hope that extraordinary human life will grow there and that other rich treasures and watering sheds will image our wondrous dark foibles in their uncultured digestive skins.

from PLEIADES IN NINE

Imagination is the venom

Imagination is the venom
passing slyly through
the vein,
real poison acts less

     painfully,
     forming high notes
     that weave across the landscape.
     It's done automatically
     all delicate intention
     missed; cushioned seat
     free from burns and
     insidious hospital logic.

To construct
the voodoo confessional
in sight of
convulsion
takes greater clarity

     & acceptance,
     beyond the wall of guarded sperm
     beyond the faint glow
     of sainted domestic
     fury.

Burning winds strip the vegetable chariot

Burning winds strip the vegetable chariot
its aim closing on advancing rocks.
Bird dreams lifting a canopy,
broken stumps of oars
swivel madly unbalanced. Savage muscle
butchering the shore:
Sun & Moon
their swell
rifles through the head,
                    lifting and crashing seas of psychotic plasma
                    about our straw anchors.
                    The knowledge is tidal; blood
                    smashes into concealed libraries
                    filling the shelves, tightening the walls,
                    gluing the books into a fetish
                    accumulator.

We can drown through our eyes
rising inside until the levels meet.
We sink between rock and air
the layer of colour is the bones
                    the brains
                    the hide
                    meat
                    and other tools, worm motor
                    powering the floodlight.

A slender doctrine

for Jack Whitehead

A slender doctrine
that leaves the ego allpowerful
but of a lower species, it mated with the tides of diffusion
haunts the shores of the ancestral island.

> In bone eminence
> the white mansion stands; its boundaries
> are beyond and enclosing the loop of time.
> The conscious laps in impotent waves
> at the sightless walls.
> All stands before memory.

Creatures are distinguished in speed trace
they are hybrids of performed incidents
living interned
and rushing through miniature gothic arteries.

Each ritual's oscillation
nets genetic bodies
weaving the trembling beast.

> Gaunt father
> stands at every highway, his illness
> becomes the ink of the raggedly drawn
> perspective. There is the link,
> between the moment
> and the whole.

Epileptic machines litter the radius.
The dented and eccentric wheel still whines
in its precarious timing.

The comedy is obtuse:
murmurs of grand storms
brewing in sealed
domestic tumours.

Small light

Small light
uneven almost forgotten
the shrouded aging laboratory flame
set into the bend
a mile.

> Saint
> poverty shredded   growing ivy
> beneath skin : prophet
> deaf roadside.
> A haunch of hessian and latin
> star pierced, transfixed
> by bread
>   & stone

There is that green washed calm
in panels of wind,
the skull
its compass fluid sick
bobbing to rest
with wind
with names.

> A direction blessed in body time.

The white vaulted future
speeds in an energy beak
projecting the path
of vision.
The building is planned, the plumb line centred
from the zygoma.

> Each section finds a swimmer
> or ascending winged animal
> dynamic in the dying light.

All along its sword shaft

All along its sword shaft
lifting skin
the city is known

its asserted love
by blinkered surgical
suggestion.

It cures all saints
even the gutter curios
are tabbed for vinegar
performance.

So they clammered for
the nerve and untanned
brain
glistening in enclosure
a peg board to string out
the city's pathology
pins and paper
marking the connections.

The eye water
is tapped
and preserved by the
hinged & tapered
priesthood

in storm umber
it shines
being the fulcrum
within the city
walls.

The assailant changes

The assailant changes
the colour of adrenal seclusion,
victim-finds tatter the storm mast
hooking perplexities while nodding in
as underdogs /
their frailties.

Only his lapels shine
after knife wipe
the towers & channels remain open
from triangular incision, the seas
will scold these wax-faced mormon
scribes,
leftovers pinning through their emulsion
slopped crowns. white mark.

Blade and eye
will vanish back
among the societies
and closed museums
left intact to
the academies.
The ships, bilious
in the illegal surf,
return to salt.

Webbed cold

Webbed cold
overspans the manipulations,
a dolt weight is the pain windup
                    the sunken land easy
                    on perspex appetite
                    the very organs streaming
                    skylines.

The prey is seen sheltering
among the principalities
& areas of maximum decay.

Reeking England spilling the paths
for her weathered sons
                    taking up axe, wild star
                    night throb with discharging
                    negatives,
the alleyways of November
spun with industrial water,
its shine
tenanted by sniper projections
set among red roofs.

                    It is the year of a winter comet
                    and the light (half moon size)
                    is magnified
                    through
                    ice

There is conversation of stepping blindly

There is conversation of stepping blindly
into candle light,
uncursed the nude tallow
smelling of whisky.

Pasture blotting up night : spasmic milk
forming over the greedy occupied pins,
tight transparent nail tissue.

Nightweight
responds with off balance
chemical nurse
seething with ancient remedies.

The drift becomes constant
our love is ill gauged against its fellow;
sticky wheels,
the hindrance in motion is the redemption;
the force of erratic lurchings
onward.

The drugs of countenance bite in.
Transforming
without distortion
the liturgy of stars.

The trunk of the street has ample burial

The trunk of the street has ample burial;
it's that false rubbing light of neon
making de-fleshing pits
among the even winded gardens.

Water season:

Heads in rain sink beneath the pavements leaving only
the sedimentary swirl of astonishment in the deserted roads.

Caked speech falls
from headstones,
future generations named.

The odd bone of post-war murder
is the weapon;
backwards,
a prepared sight, the cones filling with
hushed fire.

Lost soundings

Lost soundings
and dead crews
display their
inclinations
            fictional panic
            wireless
            in the open fronted tower
            sun warm to daze fear
                                    the sea turns white
                                    they hover in spiral.

Expediency
in predatory
glide
closes.
Its armoury of senses   Hawk chill
switching   the touchwood
& squabbling   relish cooks
for the bite   the dinghy
                               black tar
                               spits saline

            torn clumps,
            land
            tufted in fat,
            float ashore
            and gain
            weight.

Tall solar rods

Tall solar rods
arisen
that position accepted
to stoke & feed
the furnace
& run
the gully away
thick with fat

They are the molten sons
of finance, possessed
without guilt
to conclude

heart melts
making touchless
gauntlets that squeeze
the whimper from the axe.

Broken clinker
surgery in contract

loaded
gym bag
sweet,
the sleazy metal
clinking; magnums, ingrams, franchis,
sawn off
won't cool
the culture breech. The transfusions glutted in private
                    collections of hot money.

The brown won't hold the form

I.

The brown won't hold the form
even infra red only yields
hands, between the wanted
& found
pressed: the real guilt melts
in acid.

Harmony is waxed in meter
food / highrise
smog, snow, heat.
The leakage is sexual
hauling its fur
with the agitated confidence
of long term blind.

2.

Slowdrop
washed in heart room,
one pumps love;
the camera man or
the victim grinning.

The white won't hold the force
amphibious colour
nosing the very rim,
escape seems unlikely
that wanes in cynic diameter.

3.
Comic sombrero
flops out from head gland
constant wearing leaves
stigmata / the pressure ridge
aerial
this is what the cheap lenses
break in straining.

Fluid messes with glass
congeal in meat prism
blowing away all hope
of pure colour.

Driven from

Driven from
that total span,
enforced by wealth

stiffening of the mask
                    Driven to
                    the seminal scrapings
                    and wrappings of bacterial
                    bookless tribes.

                    Climatic transport
                    demands a greater gift,
                    to season in these bromide pools
                    asks bone.

internal confession

the tactile anatomy of construction
is known, the raft sits concealed in vertical pulp case.
It becomes vital
to extract
the craft
from behind the living skin.
                    First cut
                    flinches up a nail of white
                    red moves
                    the winds already drop
                    the stigmata is hewn
                    and shaved.

The distance
to settlement is marked in Mendel's signature
the road mudded against attack,
these final reflective angles
cause the immaculate vehicle
to be driven out.

They will not enter

They will not enter,
the anthropophagi.
Their fear/
tattered bats in electric vapour.

A post is driven, carved and painted.
entrance is recorded, the other is
seen deep
needle eye   wolf lore closes the dark.

Long wind
under tree
iced the eclipse of sight
it must be marked among eternal audience.
Hymns carried on banners, hidden in folds of wounds:
post rout.

Sequel

The mysterious table, varnished taste
jointed and barred with noise.

The year is wired. Hands expand, night's apparatus passes
and leaves vacant impressions.
The light drains and the volume is replaced by dream,
unsteady   tonal with delayed focus
leaving splinters that draw blood
beneath day tweed.

The raft
is the penalty and the cure
chained to steer hypnotically
across vacant oceans.

Fear is neuter

Fear is neuter
and the derelict shamans
dream out
their scorpion sex.

But the organic poisons
are washed by
tranquillizing
gas; vegetative,
looping the hard
dust island
in soaking pressure

> alternative
> horror structures
> replace the dark;
> irrational
> that swollen light,
> its reaching blade
> trawling
> the coast line.
> Fear wrecks the interior of cars
> (it will be worse on the return)
> blindfold roads
> swinging
> in sick expectancy.

Another night swim

Another night swim
topographic dream
locked in the island's heat,
unplanted personalities appear
at rough intersections;
crumbling stone
spiny plants.

The ants
are stiff & feeding
their plateau beating with fly death,
wing dissection
                hot sight
                after water vision of silent
                glide above rock carved animals
                black with size.

The present strengthens,
corners subtle
with monkey light membranes smoked with car rust.

Time bulks fluid
under vegetable hides
                pulp heads appear
                over green in the sand fields;
                blind
                watching, recording pressure

One eyed

One eyed
before the indiscreet object
fuses saxon
& photon
tunes,
played on western
carcass piano
            bull
            tremor drives the women
            and children
            into closed society.

Close to Antares
the desert serpent
cannot cut the ghost boundary,
seclusion coils
as mass breaks down
            discharging
            neutrino smog that seals
            the kiva
            & holds back the venereal tide
            of iron.

From the apparent mute

From the apparent mute
the flickering odour
dense with sympathetic drones
extracts the pain
filament   in caution
                                at the edge exposure.
                                the crumbling vertiginous
                                castellation,
                                this skin shed at last and
peeled wet   drying
raw
the violently dressed crowd
beat their fly sticks & scream
in approval.
Beyond T.V. the pathos
water gulp
emotion   Milk, word and sap
                                dissolved the caul.
                                Shaded from the heat in
                                the tiger bar'd hut the robe is given,
                                only steps away the airline's metal
its surgical   stair
tarmac
hidden in the mothering
ghost haze of the desert.
Its deafening whimper
blown clear by wind

The oil limps

The oil limps
out a secondary colour;
the chairs darken, a thick
jungle perplexity.

Tattooed across the crease
made by legs, the bleeding
pin has emptied rough hair
and exchanged glass teasing
plants.

Heat from their fur
has hardened the sleep,
the thinness evaporated
to chill the conditioned
breathing elsewhere.

The insect moves in
refusing the causeways
of mammalian seed,
it is this talismanic
force the herald carries
suspended in genetic ice.

Single approach

Single approach
gilds the collapsed density
of the necessary mileage,
after the eaten time
the true perversity
stalks ahead,
old one-eye the
obi-man.

Bull head
resigns, leaving
those in his protection
and terror at odds;
pulling the membranes
each side of the fine star line

                    weighing
                    the spores
                    that must become biographic
                    and unsanitary:
                    extravagance
                    brings
                    feline predators
                    to the open area of night.

They prowl;
saliva drawing
the chart
of possible suns
and probable nerve ways
on the arid female sand.

To seek the fires

To seek the fires
the insect
divides its wave form
imposing a hiss across its axis

 the spinal folds
 tear
 the woven symmetry
 cusps,

a powered misunderstanding of grace
causes artificial cargo to be cut
from the jungle edge.

dug hard
to make the slit
visible,

 approaching craft
 need to mate with
 this coarse-fibred diety.

Their flight path
set through cannibalism
lust talks them in.

 The mash of cultures
 thumps the jungle
 causing swollen fruit
 to fall and be skewered
 on the buzzing aerials
 of the anthropological mission.

Mantis speaks

Mantis speaks
through the office files,
in
empty air
the water and flesh mud paint
a clogged voice

> the manipulations are between vacuums
> moonpull;
> thick and hydrolic
> the nervous wall
> voice of fire vision
> is overcoated,
> daubed;
> oyster, gunmetal, ash.

this clonic lung
heaves lead future on sun rails
cruelty furnishes
the studio sound effects.

This is the hit brief
a recorder grafted under a canvas skin–hump;
sewn with gut, camouflaged with dust and directed conversations.
Its tight metal mouth
has a serpent gusset

> it is capable of devouring
> a man or a tribe.

There was a sense of yellow

There was a sense of yellow
seeming unsunned
being only placed
                    but radiating elements
                    whisp into black
                    even electricities flesh fatigues
                    being crossed by unfair celestial
                    motions
                    moving weights
                    trailing mementoes of distant speech,

so the perfumed gag moves in,
the laden wind
performing
the sexual glass amputation
creating the absolute diviner.

It becomes aware, in equal dividings
the disturbing pattern emerges; that arched internal profile.

                    Dark cells
                    devouring ancient meat
                    the understood motive becomes the deposit,
                    it places them in multiple safe transfixions.

                    Cloaks are down
                    the Mantis gathers its ink shadow
                    in cyanide light.

No milking, no calcium sea can smooth this poisonous
  angled flame.
Its own bone sanctuary
becomes the principle
               its diseased rock edge
               the pyramid lens
               to sharpen till bleeding
               the mammalian curve of birth.

In camera dinner

In camera dinner
after the prayer
roads reached about him,
Mantis
is seen in that practised gesture;
the forming of blurs on its victims eyes,
the clotting of bacterial pathways,
the roots of escape
becoming
stagnant uphill tracks
greased with suicide's irregular orbit.

Mounted for death in eyebrace
closed in hyena darkness,
smell bellies out in its heated temper
its entry / as birds crashing into vacuum.
reshaped by star-tensed permanence; spiked
outcast in predator memory.

Chant

Chant
ascending harmonies: winds distort interior,
plains duned with voice,
animal throat /
detail tornado outside the placed stones of word.

The Mantis in its crossing.
it is within a hallowed yolk of time.
its skill unstrung

        too high for tubular lungs; the thinned air
        conforming to carved plateaux.
        Blood stream dented with nitrogen shadows,
        the granite suns
        poised

over condor drops
to infinite fields
the climbing muscles harden.

Tarantula harnessed across the rust flats
the plough chromed by intension into star tool,
also bird, lizard, ape and fish
seeming washed by hard grain
cosmic tides.

WRITTEN ROOMS AND
PENCILLED CRIMES

XX

So the doctor explains calmly and with charm to the audience of artists who have come to receive technical knowledge of how they think. With elegant understatement he explains that his first task is to chemically adjust his patients' thought and speech pattern to his level of normality; he can then reach into their irregular minds and adjust them to baseline. He then with conjuror's flair isolates the lunar pons for our inspection. He weighs their singing symmetry and mechanically extends his theories onto them. The doctor's talk finishes with his aesthetic vision of imagination; his home close-ups of his garden projected in time with Mahler and Wagner, dubbed in clumsy and hesitant synchronicity.

xxi

There is a tale told of the ingenuity of an emperor or mandarin. He was engaged in an enquiry into the nature of the soul of man. He used Pavlovian techniques sharpened against his own pathological sadism. The gangrene of torture was his means of exploration. He moved beyond the usual arrogant butchery of that process: he had a subtlety and imagination that was not hindered by time or morals.

He constructed two rooms. The first was opulent beyond dreams. Fine furniture and intricate carpets graced its space. A small but rich garden adjoined the room; a delicate fountain played ceaselessly at its heart, peacocks roamed its perimeter, exotic and colourful plants curled in the scented air. Beautiful women skilled in the arts of sexual and sensual pleasure were in constant attendance. This would be the prison of the subject of enquiry.

In vicious contrast to that artificial Eden of mind and body was the other room; a harsh stone cell below ground. There is a brutish table with straps and bars, iron rings hang from the walls, a low bench is covered with all the cutlery and devices of pain. A brazier glows in one corner, making steam rise from the heavy damp walls.

The victim is brought from his luxury to this fearsome place once a day at unstated and irregular times. After his pain centre has been torn and peeled, he is washed in perfumed water, dressed in fine silks and returned to the first room.

It is obvious he will fracture along the given line of stress, the marrow of the psyche will then become exposed. It is unknown whether the emperor ever achieved his objective.

There is a third room that is neither sumptuous nor lethal. It is contemporary and can exist in your province. It is also a room made for enquiry. It is cunning in its indifference. A place constructed of cream paint, fear, and stale cigarette smoke. There is a table and three chairs. Nothing else. A curiously powerful ghost moves here, its signature is boredom, written in the absence of time. It can only be sensed in the odour given off during an enforced one-way conversation.

xxii

I have seen, heard, read, or in some way been informed about
the object that now cannot be found. Museums and libraries
have no knowledge of such a device. Scholars have never peered
into its area of operation. It simply remains a solid absolute
memory. It is not imagined and this is not a document of sly
metaphor but a print from a dislocated index. It is a circular
disc made of dry, unfired clay. A script of increasing sublimity
spirals its way from the rim across the surface to disappear
unfinished into a small hole at the centre. It is a demon trap,
to be placed in the most negative epicentre of some infested
room. The fiend will be drawn to read such an intoxicating
thing; it will become entangled in its velocity and be forced to
move through the hole. At that moment the exorcist will rush
from hiding outside the room and smash the fragile object to
pieces. The demon will be locked behind a door that no longer
exists. I can find nothing to substantiate my image, but must
watch the empty simple room that has been cleaned of the
fragments of that violent brittle momentum. Light lifts dust
from the wooden floor to breathe it against the musty heat. I
think it may be China.

xxiii

The white-hot sands became a parchment for the pale tourists
to darken, scoring like notation their desires, close to the lip
of the sea. The tide of visitors was expected and planned for
by the mob of skilled urchins who could remove with petal
fingers any possession from the sunbathing shoal. The mob
now had swollen pockets in advance of the season; pockets full
of talismans, no bigger than a coin; cyphers, shaman-cut, nimble
crosses, wheels, letters, signs, glyphs, curses. They moved in
with these on the first day of tanning. Waiting their moment
to stick the light-proof stencil to the oiled and sweating torsos
of their prey.

These signatures of retreating language would not be seen for
days. The most skilful of the urchins would return to practice
his formidable art by reregistering the stencil at exactly the
same point.

The vainest of the returning indexed hoard found and wore
their mark with glee, seeing it as a kiss to their pride. The depth
of its meaning and bite would only be felt later.

xxiv

His eyes were wrong. The lenses stretched inside the fluid to trampoline the impressions they received back to the lids. It made seeing and engaging with the world both difficult and mesmeric. Summer was a horror of drowning, being dissolved in light, a shifting assault of gigantic colours. He wore thick blue glass to keep their heat away; he carried a white stick to sign and conduct his inability to absorb.

Unlike others forms of sensory abnormality where the afflicted sense is compensated for by the growing sensitivity of the remaining others, in this case the irregularity was overpowering, creating a vivid potency that blotted out or dulled all other inputs.

Even in darkness the fluctuating eyes sought for details to rest on. This need for fine anchorage coupled with movement was almost impossible to find. In winter the falling of snow against certain lights would produce in him states of ecstasy, his being momentarily hammocked in a paradoxical weave of calm and velocity.

Shadows were his opiate, he could perceive their edges and the density of their core equally, without ever needing to know their source. He made crude experiments to generate them, constructing fumbled optics to feed his growing sensual appetite.

He worked with flame, concentrating to hold the shifting periphery in total focus while letting the pulse of tonal temperature lap deep into his core. Once while staring point blank into the halo of a candle, he was interrupted by a moth; it spiralled to the same focus, its wings producing intense subtleties of luminous movement. The final angelic incandescence filled his eyes with flickering orgasmic shadows. He needed to see more.

He became a lepidopterist; knowledge without generosity. He bred and collected hundreds of species of moth; he dissected their eyes; he measured their spirals; he passionately swallowed their burning.

The dim rooms fluttered with oddly made lights and glass tanks, larvae crawled everywhere, pupae formed encrusted surfaces that gave the flickering interior a strangely ornate, baroque quality.

This was but one track in his search, he would brave the outside world with his new confidence, seeking other visual corners, unused pockets of fuel; effects of neon on steam, storm sun on wires, any taxonomy of the violently unfocused moment; any glass-cut line spinning through time.

The summit of his quest and the ultimate satisfaction of his opthalmic sexuality came from a phenomenon that was as obvious as it was unexpected: cinema.

Thinking only of the shuttering of colour, of the harshness of cutting; one mass of complexity crashing into the next at a blink, thinking of the vulgarity of plot insisting itself upon the viewer; gimletting the emotions in the dark, padded interior. All this was an anathema to him. There was nothing there but shock for him, until he saw the scratches.

In the controlled night, quietened by ear plugs, he would be oblivious to the mass; only the dancing tendrils of light that spun and crackled privately for him would be seen, performing in a space off-screen between the projector and his insatiable mesmerised retina. The nature of the film was irrelevant, all he needed was the age of its copy and a cinema of sympathetic quality. This took him to outlying theatres where decay shivered under a coat of paint and the projector wheezed at the bulk of the film it carried. He became an expert on cinematic history; information beyond consultation.

He had found palaces dedicated to his personal fulfilment. Hours projected into days, he spent his meagre finances from the now dying insects on these orgies of light; he grew weak, a chrysalis to his passion, the optic nerve swollen to a rope.

The stunned voyeur now needed participation to gain final balance and flesh out the dusk in him. He wanted some small communication with the giants of his stimulation; he had developed a compulsion to touch their bright filament bodies, to effect their ghost brilliance. He needed some ownership to confirm himself, to vampire, by will, a gap in their inhuman energy.

He found the mechanism to the act fading in their glass tanks.

Sitting in the rising tide of scratches, the muffled sound finding chorus in his blood, the cardboard box with the hinged lid resting lightly on his knees, he awaited the moment when, totally transfixed and beyond normal control, his muscles would spasm; the box would slip, spilling the lid and the contents to the carpeted floor.

The blindsleep moths that had been packed tight would be volted into life by the pure light of the projected beam; they whirled in flock, their spiral a cyclone of shadow, their wings and their ignition momentarily caressing the raw luminous edges of the surface abrasions in the film that most of the audience were trying not to see.

They yelped in anger as their narrative was disconnected by the invasion of this irritating and unnecessary punctuation.

XXV

At the top of a tower over fractured water in flattened English fields is a locked room, kept in constant dusk. It is a cobwebbed cranial place lifted arrogantly clear of the parish mud.

The bells that hang there are empty, rheumatised into silence. Their cast-iron tongues have been removed from the weight of speech. They now lie in a measured row: one end bound by sewn leather to the collected beaks of skeletal jackdaws, the other end jointed with bone to the brass interior of cannibalised clocks.

It is not known who winds the heart of these obscure instruments or what they record in their dialless turnings.

The ticking can be heard like the sea if the enquirer presses an ear to the forged steel padlock that damply secures all access at the base of the tower.

xxvi

In another country, dazed by sun and scratched with cactus and ancient olive trees, stands a massive polished limestone cathedral. Its ponderous weight is drawn from every known mode of architecture in a naive attempt to summon classicism by volume. This stone confectionary was sited on vision; a patched and ragged woman heard angels in her melon field; a priest was told, the candle was lit. Now eighty years later a secret act is performed in the solemn unused crypt. With a viscous ink made of honey and sugar-water a script is written on the tiled floor. It is always a poetic tract filled with the light of piety.

At some distance in the dried fields is a house broken by infamy; it cannot be occupied or rebuilt. Violence and sadness haunt its crumbling stone. The same hand writes here, but the sweet ink speaks in sickness of dark things; knots of mind are unravelled in a tormented script on the pitted floor.

It has been stated that a colony of termites can be viewed as a single animal, a single consciousness. The same notion can be applied to other species of ant. In their ceaseless foraging they will enter every space, sense and feel its potential. Sugar will daze them. Its addictive protein is almost sexual; in hypnotic urgency they will pass the message, they will mass and remove every taste of it.

Once a day the script becomes visible, black with their feeding bodies. Written and erased by their radio-like passion.

xxvii

Dear Rodinsky —

I set the locust free, balanced in a privet bush in the park in red lion square, some of them were too damaged to stand, half dead, salt burnt from the taste on my lips, legs and antenna snapped off, sentenced to dust green and diesel fumes, I dont think even the birds will eat them, no point taking them back to walthamstow the chameleon and geckos would spit. I am covered in bruises and odd muscles in far corners ache like fuck but thats O.K. it gives me a taste of the locusts. I still think even in this state they carry the message, like damaged resistors or a kind of splintered wedge to keep the door open. Anyway its done and i am off to try and wash the cancerous stench of rancid butter and burnt sulphur out of the collar and cuffs of the borrowed cassock, it has to go back to hang in the vestry of st. Georges clean before the sunday service.

J.

The saints and prophets that are carved and perched on shallow pillars around the chamber were not used; their entangled, wind-swept sternness remains unbled, locked to the objects they are structured with. They were a lure. A solid manifestation of the acoustic stance of the place.

This chamber has no real place here; it is distant, its difficult proportions are outside the mind of the rest of the building. From its centre a single massive granite pillar dominates scale and intention. The stone wings it supports hold a distorted dome of glass and metal. It is blind from the war, painted out, black heat skin to hide the light inside, a paint-lidded incendiary eye. The dome is filled with sound. Whispers and concussions opalesce the shadows, causing complex resonances to seek sympathetic actions, and their organs to alibi their own generation.

The pillar in its hard-grain density pumps this down through the polished and hammered tight wooden floor. Roots of water and subway entwine, dim lights tunnelling audience away; rats like dogs running with the train, testing the speed, greedy for its accident, counting the menu; an abacus with fleas.

To this chamber the performer brings, without design, substance and risk. He brings salt, needles, sulphur, a heavy cast-iron dish, water, simple animals, oil lamps, a towel, lenses, a cast-iron horn, bread, the shabby robe of a priest, glass, butter, and five illuminated geographic globes.

A countless number of instruments and crimes could be constructed with these things; they are already vibrating between the dome and the tunnels. The operator, lost in time, tunes his identity and opens his purpose to them; he begins to draw energy and direction from the filling reservoir of his other mind.

Outside, above the door, is a clock of brass and wood, its bright chimes cannot enter the brooding somnambulistic dark where the operator washes, unaware of day or night, butter and sulphur from his tired and panicked hands.

The witnesses who can be dimly seen around the perimeter of the chamber also are losing the day while being there; some for minutes, some for hours. Some watch, some make notes, one sleeps or attempts to fuse with the sound of the subterranean river or journey; white head drawn between the wood to the illuminations of worms or trains. The pressure in the chamber can cause suspension and will dissolve normality; the witnesses feel it in their awareness of the invisible. They have seen the locust in a flute of glass quiver and transmit under the breath from the operator's lips. He, kneeling before a large map of Africa made of salt, plays the steel-capped pipe. He draws the same air back into his lungs from the body of the insects; his blood becoming enriched with myth and contagion.

The porous salt impatiently absorbs the next exhalation which passes over it on its way to the memory of the watchers.

They have heard and sensed thunder and the rhino enter the space through the dish and the horn; the operator sleeping curled around the emptiness of the one. His nightmare epileptic fever shaking the cyclonic voice from the dome to the dish. The iron horn being pulled awkwardly to his forehead, curving the spine, shoulders and head down, back high, rocking the horn along its blade edge; the torn metal stump bruising his skull. The beast is summoned through its charge, its attack. The fleshiness of head becomes a rubbery cushion between the spine and tusk. The hunched creature gores the emptiness before it, the obstinate repetitive lurch, sounding spheres, purple to black in the dome; rain; hooves shuddering the floor; a stampede of one fulfilling the muscled anger of many. The operator is held back by a hair from this minotaur velocity. The hair is frayed from the collar of the cassock that the operator is wearing. Its irritant heat welts the back of his neck, sweat blisters him, a tether to the moment. This is the only hook to engage in real time, other tendrils of action and transformation hang or float; invisible ectoplasm smoking from the dissolving man who performs the sequences while being puppeted by the place, and the chalky glass ghost dice in the hind cup of his head.

Between the clenched, hushed violence of action there is stillness. The operator washes the stains and motives from his hands in the dark water corner, black towel wrapped into hood, quietly lost, breathing slowly, waiting for the next cunning impulse to lurch him unprepared into the growing hunger of the audience.

The day is erased by exhaustion; the running, loping figure is folding back. The salt is kicked and trampled, wiped out in a plague dance, sulphur smouldering, personality crumbling. The operator disappears, broken and twitching incidents remain in the cupped voice of the dome.

from TULPA INDEX

Deinonychus (terrible claw) was a sophisticated, fast-moving dinosaur from the last reign of their kingdom. This twice-man-sized, erect marvel was a mid-point between the old and the new worlds.

Gloss of

Gloss of
oblivion
smoked bones under
Tethys ocean

> cauldron
> magma
> chrome
> side show, coin heart
> picks low tide pressings.
> Zig saws calcium, polaroids
> the marrow.

We must wear
this cloak of
dust
pinching at our wet joints,
without it the sullen garden
is oppressive, every fruit
injected with sick dead
sperm.

Deinonychus; child of the sun

Deinonychus; child of the sun
the same exchange of culinary mass
fire beyond heat,
heart and lung
expand, swallowing oxygen and flesh.

This ancestor of Christ holds surgery
deep and secret around word.
Knowledge is only velocity
blood thick with information
to be squeezed in the brain.

He is claw, arrow, spear,
bone tool box of savagery.
Deinonychus would not enter any ark of vision.
He remains to snap at the rain &
rend the belly of tidal wave.

It's the arrogance of satan
refusing to let his bones be scattered
or saved in a morbid dogma zoo.

Adam could not be seen

Adam could not be seen
in that vulgar culture park.
But he was there sealed in
its garden centre.
At the conscious perimeter
a horned truck mentality
nudges the invisible wires
pulling a fresh wound
open in the inner
memory,
               stagnant fishing
               the outer beasts need his fame.
               but only to rewash
               their protein
               haloes.
Deinonychus
is another
prototype.

Tethys craft

Tethys craft
submerged
upon ribs
buried, mud flank; we cannot force
the periscope high enough;
the neck of protoplasma
inclines to community warmth

        pre-mammary nipple
        a fiction in mineral
        cleated in a salt cave.

Ocean sunken
the temple is
a body,
vast
picked and nudged clean by nutrition
geomantically structured
by pressure,
clenched &
dropped by
moon gauntlet

        through it
        the sun's massive sexual
        greed flays
        wave upon wave,
        but cannot reach deep tidal
        entrails solid
        with black
        microscopic lusts.

The truth is

The truth is
that Harryhausen
is as close as Darwin;
rubber coated seconds bend,
courtly needs are cracked in the frame.
It was the lion's roar in reverse
that was heard in volcanic winds.

Sraetic sandwich
peels in the Roentgen heat
man dances in camera
(the beast is added later)
It is the ghost ritual learnt
from the chromosome dice,
each race waits
on the caution line
of shadow.

The matte box is a time
nut
celestial in construction
operated by an opisthonic
tune.

It began with all loutishness, behold that it ends

'It began with all loutishness, behold that it ends
with angels of the fire and ice.'

But the mirror must occur first,
the reflection beyond social sight.
Silver flakes peel
& drop in blackish light,
their foil marks
rents in the ionisphere

> angry solar arms
> reach down.
> Polar scabs are picked
> loose
> (frost bite)

Pentangular
prisms can no longer
contain their love
caution is split
in the
fireplace.

Deinonychus smelt the same brimstone, felt the same
wind in advantage of ice. He did not scurry in
spermicidal panic.

Pink smear

Pink smear
crouched
under incubation
umbrella

on that early carbon raft
lashed with tars & tissue collected
from the slip stream.
Rain
pits the time storm
using the water to
shred & wither
the genetic
yeomanry.

Just above
his water-logged brain
Deinonychus
sees
this.

The line between himself, the plague carrier
& God
is narrowing;
it is a temperature
chart rising
to heat.

Deinonychus did not know

Deinonychus did not know
how vicious his resurrection
would be.
In the sightless moment
it takes flesh to ascend to stone

          he had transformed;
          locked
          in a mineral topiary,
          distilled to tincture.

With simian joy
we dig our greedy hand
downwards,
lured to mainline it works
as root pulling up richer & richer fluids.
Our speed glares in one direction
and cannot see or feel his ancient
& agile shadow
waiting
to step
out of
exile.

Eugene Marais scattered himself with a shotgun on a remote farm near Pretoria in March 1936. Before that his solitude and addictive vision twisted through poetry, law, and natural science. This small patch of word is a chant to him.

'Clutching the book, consumed by the excited possibility of meeting the magic-maker alone, he went to the house, found the room, knocked. There was no answer. He tried the door, it was unlocked. He entered cautiously. The room was dank with disorder. And there was a strange smell. He put the book down and fled.
Many years later after Marais' death Weiner was a medical student at St. George's Hospital in London. He was handed a sample drug with a very queer smell. Instantly he had a vivid recollection – a total recall of a room somewhere. He struggled to identify the room, and knew it must be somewhere in South Africa. Then it came to him – Marais' little room. The drug was morphine.'

ROBERT ARDREY.
From his introduction to
'The soul of the ape'.

Marais gave the earth his spoon

Marais gave the earth his spoon.
Refusing to crush the motion
he extracts from nerve ends
& adds them to his limited supply
of opiates.

All this is previous
to the deep sniff
of cordite (that by the vicious
sexual laws of proximity
is aimed.)
        Each fibre
        of plant
        sand
        earth
        colours the hand of the most casual observer.
        This is Africa
        and the heavy dutch tongue
        nailed under the heat dries
        forcing the language to skree
        past dead saliva ducts,
        outside
        in the burning oxygen it cannot even be heard.

Its too early
for the voice of the mouth here;
the throat is the jug of fluidity.

Marais gives his spine to the mantis

Marais gives his spine to the mantis
who counts its cracks, stains & ridges
seeing there the wheat cuneiform of Europe.

It must be posted across water
or used
              arid mace
              against paternal cartridge.
              powdered in marrow dust; broken
              on a neotonous sphinx,
or used
              fence post
              rigid in synaptic decision
              a strength across the plain.
              Rhinoceros, wildebeest, ox.

It must be stolen
              wrapped in paper
              and lost.
              The compulsion
              to obscure.

Marais gives the water his neuron

Marais gives the water his neuron
posing a problem of need,
using it to span ancestral tides.

It's impossible to cross
the bridge set down by desire
it is both/ the thin twig placed
            across accident to test
            our greater need and
            outstretch into a day
            the instinctive hand.

        also/ the medieval hunchback
            sprawl over spoken waters,
            in the spiritual cause
            and effect, hybrid
            tutors are bolted against
            the skin mat, so we cannot
            step back to focus
            or fall.

Marais gives the messenger his eye

Marais gives the messenger his eye.
It is quickly smuggled
past the enamelled fanned air of the cities
and greedily buried
in the veldt.

Towers are spat up
in blind monument
around the orb;
a seed egged
deep in luminous
oppression.

Marais gives his need to the jackal

Marais gives his need to the jackal
who with canine truth devours the outer skin,
the denser meat is turgid
with congealed force.
A more gravelled digestion is needed.
Hyenas
close
around the drawn circle of hope,
                                        they cross
                                        and enter
                                        a hub flesh of fear.
Dominance takes the greater share
becoming sick in later vulture light.

Nightmass
ushers the whimper, bringing candle eye
weaklings of the tribe,
they take a tighter nourishment from the ring, and thrive.

Marais gives his hands to the wind

Marais gives his hands to the wind
so that the ghost experiments and abuses
can be conducted on a larger scale.

*'take a steel plate a few feet wide and higher than
the termitary, drive it right through the centre of
the breach you have made in such a way that you divide
the wound and the termitary into two separate parts.
One section of the community can never be in touch with
the other, and one will be separate from the queen's cell.'*

In that case
force of existence spins a neutrino light through
the metal ignorance
potency that cannot
even see 'obstacle'.

Across the secure lawn
steel plates
are set on angry oiled springs
window lids
        that guillotine up
                cutting the day
                & firing the screams.
                Hair triggers
                are wired into radar
                and pressure pads

                Cocktails
                are split
                by the crossing of an ant
                or the cast of the wind.

Marais gives the flies his pigment

Marais gives the flies his pigment.
In a dry albino flight their contrast
is lost, the target
cannot be found in the dazed ring
of irritation.

Sound too excepts
this skin,
curling its swollen weight
into tissue hiss
perfect for fluorescent
commerce attack
> but the past
> is obvious
> in the bush, its dead food glare
> is open on night skin.
> The simple thing
> forgets to fly
> in the dense animal air,
> drunk
> it becomes a sign
> & is smeared casually away.

The burnt drug

The burnt drug
carpets the room
clots the bed
& drives
extremities down
                no bird
                can say
                in sight song
                its non-colour.
The child carries
the scent of a constructed wilderness
the rest of its life
                no insect
                is
                harmless
                after exposure
                to open sky.
Birth test
run from
gelatinous mass
boiled to standstill,
                one-roomers quench their centrifugal
                violence on that;
                Marais gives the prison
                his spoor.
                No animal
                can take it
                & plants will only draw
                thin salts
                from it,
                carefully.

WRITTEN ROOMS AND PENCILLED CRIMES

xxviii

Cloyed green curtains and the uneven porous palms of a crumbling tiled floor support and hood these waxen virgins from the adolescent light of the Boboli Gardens.

Tucked in the throat of this palace of dust skins and sewn wings is the *Museo della Specola*: an anatomical landscape where blood never flowed. These spurious caged meats never tasted the excitement of adrenalin or the silken glaze of endorfins.

They are stained ghosts of puppeted violence. Heavy in a docile cunning of inflexibility.

They are at one with their surroundings, vampired oils in horror of sunlight. They must remain under this torpid neon caul that offers a harsh amplified dusk and imparts the impassive charm of a long empty bar.

They were born of pressure and fire: an exchange of heats, cooling flesh and heated wax. Cadavers brought for the sculptor/surgeons to transform. The hands of Sussini and the assistants working in mirror, casting closed negatives of that which has been peeled open. Strength of fingers tearing, teasing, easing apart, modelling damp cold clay to stiffening plaster, all moisture locked. White hand: the powders have silenced the communications natural to waters. Cupped, set. Inside-out seen through touch, the fingers colour sinewed expression with leech knives of wood, files, sandpaper.

Time tilts solids, decay flannels touch, giving secluded wax a dignity to confuse the flies and worms who are lost in their banquet, tasting dough in the honey. All matter crosses, blood is smeared to wax, clay smeared to bone: a studio-passion washed of callousness and perfumed in the academy.

Dr. Spitzner has also curated surgical mummeries of wax. Quibert gives a salacious voice to these hidden works. 'In one scene of caesarian incision, the woman's legs are tied at the ankles with a white scarf, while disembodied men's hands cuffed in black and starchy white come from nowhere to wield sponges and scalpel, as they cut between the folds of the patient's frilly nightdress.' From these relentless fictions I have netted a storm. I have bred hands. Incubated them in gloves of sulphur. Coaxed harsh nubile bone to invert itself. Carved them from occulted stones of lost intentions. Bathed them in milk under the swollen names of angels. And on that distant night unleashed them; a sending, a maelstrom of many where only one was needed. Tinder nails bite sparks from the walls in their passing, their velocity echoes stars in rain water cobble stones, a scatter over darkness, a flutter into dust; right hand, left hand, the prey being sensed, a warmth inbetween. Closing.

The square, the street, the food importers, the school. The prey hollowed in gin, seeking a name, a word. The passion of their hit is unknown, a tidal wave of touch, wearing the victim. They that did not engage will run wild, fiercing themselves into everything.

Months, years, decades later stains of their eruption will be found. A can of tinned meat taken from the square will be politely sliced in a rural shop somewhere. The razor disc blade will cut circular slivers of bone from the claw at its centre. Books in the school will not open because of the blind dead thing snatching at their interior. Walls removed to make way for new confines will shudder under the last twitch of a manic splintered embrace. Some may still be alive inside the bones, the mittens of the families named as suspects.

xxix

It is a cold night that limps towards dawn. There should be a wind that twitches and pulls at the tented cloak, that covers the watcher from head to toe; but it is on the outside now, and this machine cannot yet divide the boundary.

It is a camera made from many things clipped from the corporeal body of indolent seclusion. This tiptoed skeletal inquisitor leans into the cocooned face of its operator: seamed jowl to hinge by the long mantle of dark cloth. They appear to stare at a neutral wall in this industrial blankness of the new brewery building. Stagnant beer, oil and cleaning fluids run between their legs and wed them damply to the place. The endless teeth of bottles are quiet on their mechanical steel road. Distant traffic murmurs loosely rubbing at the lost noise.

Hunger is its film; stretched in a sewn box of compressed earth. Metal foil stings the clods together in an arid pellicle of containment. There is a force in this magnetised cavity of solid expectation that screams, momentum in its void. Its constructed size is equal to womb or brain pan; it gulps, needing to sauté some kin to light against its greased sides; to swallow a stone of blood. Its lens is the shrivelled remains of an orb, stolen from a museum of victims. It is elegantly strung, between tentacles of fine oiled paper and gleaming black pins, in a cone of deeply frozen sperm.

This permafrost optic is without focus or the ability to blink. It jitter-glares from the lid of its intimate lazaret into the cracked area that was once a back yard, a dripping, sidling place: extreme: a nobility of squalor. The watchers are straining for a woman who is a pendulum in an incidental history. Mindplate; seeing her pinwheeling from her centre on a spindle of hatred, a surprising brightness to the ochred weariness of the place.

The warm sluggish smell of the cats' meat suppliers that occupied the front of the house filled that erstwhile night, still cupping the remnant of its sullen day. This conjures another boundary – to definition. Temperature.

Adjustment can only occur here, gland valve is hushed,

lapped tongue stapled to boxwood; a conduit for shunting degrees of need, equalizing condensation and sweat to clear the view.

It is long past the hour of event. The hourly changing angels clock the shift, ringing echoes of disappointment in the cloak. Disintegration threatens the camera, its cellular buckles and cramped tails unwinding, moving apart in a shrugged, comic bewilderment.

The ghosted intention is all that remains, desperate to obscure itself as the workers begin to arrive. It has become a pencilled stand-in for the other, a superimposition from another mythology that makes any focus beyond tenable sight.

The only thing to process in a tray of future salts is a blur.

xxx

The passenger's stories of his family's distant savagery were believable. Equally convincing was the image of an isolated childhood only stimulated by fear and violence.

It was when he explained that he had been born without feet or hands, and that the present extremities were grafted on at a later date, that credibility was stretched nervously over the thin bone of panic. The countryside we rattled through had that inconsolable dreary aspect that makes it impossible to watch with any degree of conviction.

The suffocative reds and browns of the train compartment equally gave no prospect of pleasurable focus and vacant disconnection. This madman was the only centre in the locked stutter of communication. My hopefully absent gaze ignited another swollen monologue. His mother once owned a piece of glass, taken from the broken window of an unnamed country house. The image of a screaming woman was trapped in it; if held before a paraffin lamp in December it was possible to hear a faint cry.

The ear is the most vulnerable of all organs of perception; this is embarrassingly amplified by its own total lack of expression. The blank curled flaps give no sign of irritation, joy, tiredness or excitement, while filling the head full of bubbling and layered signs and triggers. The rest of the shifting mass called face is forced to overcompensate or attempt to imitate that same impassive gristle of the ear, but to fail miserably.

It is in these stenotic rushings that the mind digs deep and stumbles in its archive for a key to escape, lightning glimpses of objects and actions are tipped for rummage; any cruciform or soap gun that can be held up in projection of the uncoming attack. The unconscious passes its chaotic arsenal in scent across the waiting hand. Against these two hours of numbing awareness an axe is grasped; Nürnberg, circa 1650, an abysmal thing for execution, dense in its iron brutality, off-balance in its single purpose. But it is its detail that is unholstered to give balm to this time, its detail that is grasped white in the hand.

Hidden in a carefully made recess in the wooden shaft is a pair of scissors; they are intimately slotted there for convenience so they will not fall loose and give offence. The pedantic headsman would use these to trim the hair from the back of the victim's neck so nothing would hamper the sullen arc of his blow or blows.

xxxi

She was attractive, quite young with three children, the curator said. These details added a linctus of curiosity to the cauldron of astonishment that the object created. It sat in a fluid tank behind a wall of labelled glass. Wooden cases of dense brown gave the room its overall gloom. We were searching for the lead worker's foot – the curator had mislaid it somewhere – when we found its feminine twin.

The foot was solid nexus of lead, flesh and leather. The unfortunate worker had stepped back into a pool of the molten metal and rapidly pulled his bone peg out; his dripping foot-shoe being both the cast and the mould of itself.

The object we now looked at was also a cast, a meticulous impression made without heat. This glossy lump was ten inches long and about six inches in circumference at its thickest point. It was a human stomach cast in hair. A compacted coagulate of long strands, eaten until the organ was full and food could no longer squeeze past its baleen-like garden. When the surgeons removed it, it refused to yield its form, holding stoically to the physical memory of its host.

She can be imagined, sitting with or near her children, perhaps gazing out towards a Vermeered window distractedly pulling and mouthing her hair.

xxxii

The haloes first started to appear at the end of an acrid summer, which cooked stains and scars deep into the pavements of the city. Human, vegetable and animal fluids boiled fast to the insomniac grit screen of streets.

The haloes could not be seen at that time, their circular negative hum was the only sign: a ring of silence drawn off from the continual ache of noise. The floating absence was localised and so pure it could print itself in stillness on the quivering surface of an eardrum. These minute afterburns in both ears constructed a rod on which the mind would perch. Those stigmatised by the gift became impregnated with the disengagement of Lazarus; carefully hearing the world spin away from humanity, poised nervously for flight.

The haloes became visible as the light singed into autumn. Children and derelicts found them first; the panic and laughter drew pilgrims to the backstreets, waste lots and previously ignored penetralia of the city.

They hovered against gravity and matter, obviously substance, but a ghost version; irreverent atoms performing outside their memory. A hand passed through them would be subtly powdered for a second or two without causing any disintegration of their form.

Fear hit when the transient spinning dust was identified. Cocaine, valium, morphine, amphetamines, heroin, all the extracts and tinctures of oblivion, control and chemical interference were found. Each halo composed of a single drug, each in its own orbit of poison.

Dealers and prescriptionists could not steal it with their nibs; the users could not be crowned with its intoxication nor could they bleed it away for their needs. The spectres remained aloof and uncuttable, distant to their tribes of disciples.

After tourism faded the phenomena became an embarrassment to the authorities. They erected temporary screens that soon became splintered by the picking of curiosity; they built and manned barricades that became worn away by finance and boredom. Finally they bricked them in, walls and bunkers hiding the inexhaustible, dismal luminescence. The sealings gave the angular city a distortion of organic growth. Previous arteries now being blocked forced new roads and spaces to be opened. A different map was growing inside the metropolis, it was drawing its own ancestor; a vast circle of reinvented causeways and curving directions.

Occasionally a brick would be removed to confirm continuity, it did – and increased the solidity of despair; the populace began to understand, somewhere deep inside, the indifference of the haloes. They knew these traces, vivacious in their guilt, would outlive them and their home; that they would glide in their place over the rubble, even in the cinders and the vacuum.

from PLEIADES IN NINE

They nestle

*'Death hath not only particular stars in heaven, but
malevolent places on earth, which single out infirmities,
and strike at our weak parts; in which concern passage
and migrant birds have the great advantage.'*

They nestle,
a smear in the dark.
Pyramid
target centred,
the brain mites crystallising
under desiccated morse,
            shutter peeling
            circumcision.
            All hope for the vision
            lost
            each year.

There is knuckle ash
in the duke's hutch;
the weeded depository broken and fungus welped.
These blocks of polished dead: wax
and water

the wings
are stone
& shape the grudge.
They beat out of speed
with light,
the time illuminated at
the same position in the
loop.

On returning
the fear is decapitation by feather,
also the woman has dreamed of my blindness;
the pitiful opening
of glass doors.

This shelf in

'It was a very safe place because it was
too shallow to be a den for lions or any other
predators, too open to be nest for rats and
too windy for insects. He laughed and said
that it was an ideal place for men, since
no other living creature could stand it.'

This shelf in
the circle can act for us
tucked in the cleat
of matter
            solar currents shave
            the star bristle, dropping the towel
            on ice floor.

Mid planet pressure
causes drought, chipping the safety catches
on the polar rim.

The polished ecliptic field
smokes over
in protection, too much fear
is withdrawn
& the force lines weaken, taps can't
                        flood the
                        dissolving layers
                        and the rink
                        glides apart.

From its oiled prism
concealments ooze, paper kites of insane backstreet
magicians attract their attention

                        beyond that the focus
                        closes; heat systems, tide pulls
                        the entire atomic gruel
                        active in nourishment.

Burning granite hour

'The West stairway was occupied by wild animals.
From the top stair to the bottom stair it was
given up to antelopes, hyenas, cats (two stairs for these)
reptiles and saurians, apes, gazelles, marmots, the lion
and the elephant.
After the sixth step came the trees from the baobab
to the lannea acida, and on each of them were the insects
commonly found there today. The ninth stairway was occupied
by men and fish.'

Burning granite hour
wearing
low ebb: 3 a.m.
        Standing from this construction,
        a solution of rain and star
        ammonic to make the heart whine and twitch.
        They form in spite
        of cold and the skeletal guardian.

Micro clusters spill
from the bleeding,
smeared across the glass pyramid
beating in blind solar winds.
Biotic stemming is achieved on the vicious undead walls.

The angered coat of life
sulks
myotic plasma feeds spinally; snake of nerves.

        In the retreating gallons of night
        the salt levels rise
        the stone glistens with gristle ore,
        flood gushes from its peak.

Low coastal town is fused on its outskirts
drinking stops, television blooms out,
poultry radio gags.

That scale held, towards newsprint grey
searise   iceslip
wooden island in mountain form.

Premonition: woman slung

Premonition: woman slung.
They drip
into feudal mountains
    tongues wrapped in bitumen,
    their lead diving suits crushing
    & rocking,
    slow motion tremors within all life.

Stellar fish
grip approaching waves
to describe speed.

From the evaporating pouch new bones are pressed,
injected with the oil of coition
hammered by distant X-Ray
matted by pumice dust
    seared round with the insistent
    volcanic boa
    wrapped about the sense trunk.
    Tempered
    by mad sun

No love knits the blood
it is asexual, a clean pressure
constant.
Reforming the lines, denting the slippery helix,
climbing.

Life breeds

Life breeds
in any mistake
given half the
chance;
tendril plasma hooking
to witless bone

                no cure
                in the painted dams
                their hinges and folds
                are constructed of treacherous
                organic tissue.
                No aid
                in ancestral armour
                their dead hands have
                grown against opening
                hollow and defiant.

Any token is layered
and cannot again be laid
easily aside; the theft
of death's ownership
leaves luminous
cancer marks
in migration

                it will graft
                itself to your spine
                and share that potency
                & blood
                amputate it and your dying
                is formed
                in arrowhead.

from TULPA INDEX

Old Proteus blind in his cave

Old Proteus blind in his cave
has drawn a line / stabbing the broken
veins or dry Bic pens in the mould.
Red ink, blue ink.
Its route has excepted the market place
but left other generations to arrange the
venal chronology
& repaint the plague carts.

It runs close to the temple wall
the pace bleeds / inside pocket
notation lost in tackiness;
all substitutes
for blood against the heart,
in the cup,
over the shower floor (drinking chocolate)
monochrome is the sickly taste.

Beyond there
the colour runs to mud,
& the direction is splintered by traffic.

The font

The font
was a hollow laid out of flesh-hood,
a watering place lured
from marrow.
All kinds
of bugs
foster here, scratching thin
dead light
                        sulphur
                                    peering
to read
a menu
of transformation.   too rich
in this spatial fire dream of air.   We smoke on it,
shuffle
& stagger over
the charred chromosomes, that could have been
glued & painted
to make some kind of Chaplinstick, bent
but white in the dark.

Entrance

Entrance
suspended over the hunting fields,
not death, the living vine
calligraphs subtle anatomy
that cannot be called
heart.

Blood
will not be strangled
in prosaic diagram (the home,
the work) its heat
wallows menacingly
in a thin glass
chalice.

> Simple
> splinter along the doctor line,
> drug putty
> from warm dusk
> pocket
> wont, cannot harness
> the ripe pressure of
> that thunderous colour.

They cock

They cock.
The words
outside the sanctum door, only
a cave,
the horned and triple eye
stays intact.

Stars circle
their stilts curling red dust from the ground,
a drunken walk.
Amid the open chests
and weighted skulls, the whole calcium kellogg pack
sprinkled in removable museum sugar
stirs a clue.

The ambush grows
weary of waiting; in the silence
holding the urine tight
hot,
attack
sickly gunfire / academic belligerence
echo through the stasis years,
the mould of the eighth day cracks open
showing the last gift
the grail
of opiate ignorance

Fur hammers

(white)

Fur hammers
my hands
turned inside out   against touch
boned and timorous   Open: they web urbane
a modified hare   suspicion, factory leather,
entranced   crushed veins, wax.
& matted
to a teak syrup road,
clasped in halogen   Closed: They conceal
to be reworked   migraine warmth of another
in a crucible   body, ghosted to a leash
of wolf breath   of voracious scent,
                                                a vespered stain, heat,
                                                touch, musk.

(red)

or masked   Folded: a box
in arcadian pockets   a nut, harder than
a pet weal fingered in   incubi.
poached security

Divergence opens the appetite

*'In Australia there is a parrot which plucks the wool
from sheep to line its nest. By chance it acquired a taste
for flesh and now it attacks sheep for their meat.'*

Divergence opens the appetite
morals scurry deeper into the culture,
lice-speed keeps them from the aerial eye.
Innocence is a carpenter's skill, miles from
the blood-stained hutch of families.
Nothing can step cleanly out,
twigs and brambles clotted
with birth
and desire
fuck the wedding gown.

It's billed as a high
light-filled ascendence; renaissance play.

Death rolls in the aisles
incapable of holding his ticket.

On reaching

On reaching
& finding,
vapour sainted
magnitude
        below sun line
           lost.
           The mother cord is also
           the trip wire, spilling
           in stage effect
           the possibility to see.
Our sagged
retina is no world map
           fly posted in dug-out
           to convince ominous
           shadows of their
           sacred geology.

Feeding generosity

Feeding generosity
from solitude
        nailed by description, heads broken away
        cowardice holds the claw; its only plausible
        act. Petty injections puncture the fleshfire,
        doubt is a calvinist breaking the needle
        casually while rearranging poetic furniture
        to collect light.
        It must be against the sun,
        steel is the tongue
        only in safe domestic pulpits.

Cynic is
fleshed from collapse.
            Wanting to swallow the hand and
            tear out
            the entire map of affection; to comb
            it clean
            offering it up for more meaningful
            carnage.
            The trap/the need
            brought about by conditioned survival
            humid mother nurtures
            anabatic surface nerves
            from an obese mould of fears.

We speak

We speak
those of us who
still can
      of identity
      but
      not the baggage names
      of isolation
      that is a putty blessing
      over the vice lips,

      wrenching
      a morphic finality,
      levering spine
                apart
                      with credit card.

Crossing the rills

Crossing the rills
coming through that great expanse
of mind, couched at horizon ilk
to eyeline we meet
                    a father and ask
                    does thy blood sickle this straw
                    in which we scratch & weave a home?
                    The reply
                    is daunted in wind,
                    hushed to mum
                    a folklore of frayed
                    detail sealing the gap.
Once more in our orphanage
of congealed doubts we consult the moor;
snow & rain
fresnal the view
agreeing on the solitude and calm of now.

The dream is without

The dream is without
plugs
unknown mixture of wiring,
taking the chance
face on to fusing
the entire building

Smoulder clay
arced
under the illumination
of safe
power
                              or
                                    neurotic netting
                                    wire against
                                    a darker sky
                                    a sleep without terminals
                                    to run
                                    wild fish
                                    its station on another
                                    rim
                                    parallel
                                    to food chain.

Oak saddle

Oak saddle
asks for water,
no charity
   just a desperate need to rot
   in this fringe of abused ground,

   up from
   fumic grass to hinterlands
       where
       displacement in fluids
       is hung in metal; baptism
       is fonted in iodine.

Sensual mercury
is in envious opposition
to heavy sugars   & centrally heated
           liqueurs
(conjunctiva) wax shawl
sarcastically draped in defence of small learnings.

Endless
the gummed observations of
upholstered poets
suffocated
with no clear water left
     to lick
     zinc & silver implants
     or even
     their urban postal
     wounds.

Bibled the simple axe

Bibled the simple axe
is cloaked for quiet
turmoil,
   its lithic halo a shy
   in this weird
   field of murder;
   the fungal glow
   shelling out a fragmentary
   grace
   over
   the looming pathology
          dusk,
   running in solution
   a kind
   of distant water
   unlike adrenaline
   is frozen across the blood;
           iced to lens.

Raw from starburn

Raw from starburn
& fresh from woman power
                    only too willing
                    to touchstone
                    &
                    sing,
                    before shedding the space
                    & forgetting
                    the meat
                    to remember
                    a tantric
                    wing
                    husked in a distant
                    fallopian
                    cloud.

By now

By now
a mat of tossed
and cooling cells
is lubbered
beneath our
foxed & comic
bed.

There, it dreams
of flight;
airways woven in skinflint
curling to
shores
unspumed by
human rise.

UNCOLLECTED

Up in the ideal trees

Up in the ideal trees
they found him,
at monkish play
in the wind
the suited bone.

Being here

Above the well of Jacob. Whitechapel, April 1989

Being here
after following the spokes,
so long, hand over
hand
climbing to the centre
& it does not move.
Stubborn, the clouds
and the child
who will not be born here
but chooses to grip so
to be
thresholded back
by holding,
hand over
hand to
here.